Stirling Bridge
& Falkirk 1297–98

William Wallace's rebellion

Campaign • 117

Stirling Bridge & Falkirk 1297–98

William Wallace's rebellion

Pete Armstrong • Illustrated by Angus McBride

Series editor Lee Johnson • *Consultant editor* David G Chandler

First published in Great Britain in 2003 by Osprey Publishing,
Midland House, West Way, Botley, Oxford OX2 0PH, UK
443 Park Avenue South, New York, NY 10016, USA
Email: info@ospreypublishing.com

ISBN-13: 978-1-84176-510-5

Editor: Lee Johnson
Design: The Black Spot
Index by Alan Thatcher
Maps by The Map Studio
3D bird's-eye views by John Plumer
Battlescene artwork by Angus McBride
Typeset in Helvetica Neue and ITC New Baskerville
Originated by The Electronic Page Company, Cwmbran, UK
Printed in China through World Print Ltd.

07 08 09 10 11 14 13 12 11 10 9 8 7 6 5

For a catalogue of all books published by Osprey Military
and Aviation please contact:

NORTH AMERICA
Osprey Direct, C/o Random House Distribution Center,
400 Hahn Road, Westminster, MD 21157, USA
E-mail: info@ospreydirect.com

ALL OTHER REGIONS
Osprey Direct UK, P.O. Box 140, Wellingborough,
Northants, NN8 2FA, UK
E-mail: info@ospreydirect.co.uk

www.ospreypublishing.com

Artist's note

Readers may care to note that the original paintings from
which the colour plates in this book were prepared are
available for private sale. All reproduction copyright
whatsoever is retained by the Publishers. All enquiries
should be addressed to:

Scorpio Gallery,
PO Box 475,
Hailsham,
East Sussex
BN27 2SL
UK

The Publishers regret that they can enter into no
correspondence upon this matter.

KEY TO MILITARY SYMBOLS

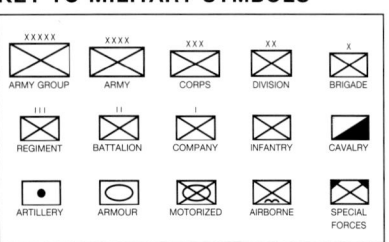

CONTENTS

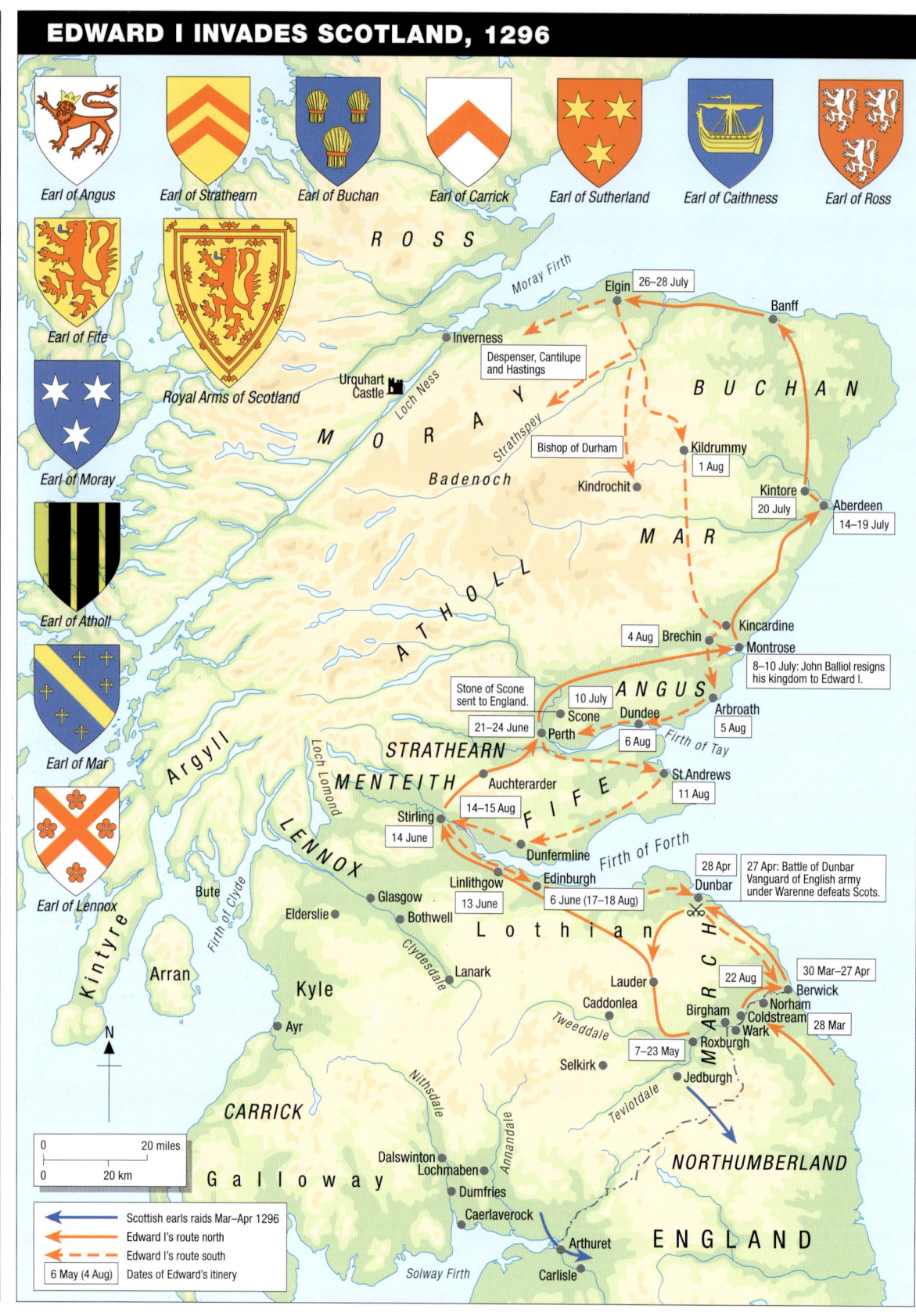

EDWARD I INVADES SCOTLAND, 1296

Earl of Angus

Earl of Strathearn

Earl of Buchan

Earl of Carrick

Earl of Sutherland

Earl of Caithness

Earl of Ross

Earl of Fife

Royal Arms of Scotland

Earl of Moray

Earl of Atholl

Earl of Mar

Earl of Lennox

R O S S

Moray Firth

Elgin 26–28 July

Banff

Inverness

Despenser, Cantilupe and Hastings

Urquhart Castle

Loch Ness

B U C H A N

M O R A Y

Strathspey

Bishop of Durham

Kildrummy 1 Aug

Kintore 20 July

Aberdeen 14–19 July

Badenoch

Kindrochit

M A R

A T H O L L

Kincardine

4 Aug Brechin

Montrose

8–10 July: John Balliol resigns his kingdom to Edward I.

Stone of Scone sent to England.

10 July

A N G U S

Arbroath 5 Aug

21–24 June

Scone

Dundee

Perth

6 Aug

Firth of Tay

S T R A T H E A R N

M E N T E I T H

Auchterarder

St Andrews 11 Aug

14–15 Aug

F I F E

Stirling 14 June

Argyll

Loch Lomond

L E N N O X

Dunfermline

Firth of Forth

28 Apr

27 Apr: Battle of Dunbar Vanguard of English army under Warenne defeats Scots.

Linlithgow 13 June

Edinburgh

6 June (17–18 Aug)

Dunbar

Bute

Glasgow

Eldersglie

Bothwell

L o t h i a n

M A R C H

22 Aug

30 Mar–27 Apr

Berwick

Arran

Kyle

Clydesdale

Lanark

Lauder

Birgham

Norham

Coldstream

28 Mar

Ayr

Caddonlea

Tweeddale

Wark

Roxburgh

7–23 May

Selkirk

Jedburgh

CARRICK

Nithsdale

Teviotdale

N O R T H U M B E R L A N D

Dalswinton

Lochmaben

Annandale

0   20 miles

0   20 km

G a l l o w a y

Dumfries

Caerlaverock

Arthuret

E N G L A N D

Solway Firth

Carlisle

Kintyre

N

	Scottish earls raids Mar–Apr 1296
	Edward I's route north
	Edward I's route south
6 May (4 Aug)	Dates of Edward's itinerary

ORIGINS OF THE CAMPAIGNS

The lion rampant of Scotland was first used in the time of William 'the Lion' (1143–1214), the bordure of fleurs de lys appeared during the reign of his son, Alexander II (1214–1249). The double tressure flory-counter-flory was first used on the great seal of Alexander III in 1251. (drawing by Pete Armstrong)

SCOTLAND WITHOUT A KING

The night of 18 March 1286 was to prove a fateful one for Scotland. In Edinburgh, after a day spent attending to affairs of state, King Alexander III of Scotland dined and drank with his counsellors. At length his thoughts turned to the attractions of his French wife the beautiful Yolande de Dreux whom he had married the previous October. She was at Kinghorn in Fife and Alexander resolved that he would ride the 22 miles to be with her despite the blackness of the night and the atrocious weather. As he and his companions made their way along a winding cliff-top path above the Firth of Forth the king became separated from his attendants. His horse stumbled and threw him and in the morning he was found on the shore, below the cliffs, with a broken neck – Scotland was without a king.

In retrospect Alexander's long reign was seen as a golden age of peace and prosperity but his achievements were undermined by his failure to provide Scotland with a legitimate male heir. His first wife Margaret, daughter of Henry III of England, died in 1275 and their children, two sons and a daughter, did not long outlive her. It had been hoped that Alexander's marriage to the young Frenchwoman might produce a male heir to rectify the situation but his untimely death left instead a sickly three-year-old as heir to his throne. She was Alexander's granddaughter whose mother, the queen of Eric II of Norway, died in 1283 giving birth to Margaret, the 'Maid of Norway', last of the royal house of Canmore. A council of regency was appointed to administer the kingdom in the name of Queen Margaret in distant Norway and a deputation was sent to Edward I, who at this time was embroiled in affairs in Gascony, to inform him of the situation in Scotland. No doubt the king considered the implications of events but at the time he took no action. When he returned to England, in the late summer of 1289, Edward proposed a marriage between his infant son, Edward of Caernarvon and the Maid of Norway. The Scots assented to this in the Treaty of Birgham in 1290 though the terms of the agreement warily insisted that the realm of Scotland was to continue as an entirely separate and independent kingdom.

But it was all for nothing as Margaret died shortly after landing in Orkney leaving the succession open again and bringing forth a rash of 'Competitors' eager to stake their claim to the vacant throne. Realising the danger of this situation and the possibility of civil war, the Scots nobles invited the intervention of Edward I. In May 1291 Edward met the Scots on the Border at Norham on Tweed and informed them that he would judge the various claims to the throne though they must acknowledge him as overlord of Scotland and, to ensure peace, surrender the Royal Castles of the kingdom into his keeping. In the face of Edward's army

ABOVE **The Great Seal of John, King of Scots (1292–1306) bearing the inscription IOHANNES DEI GRACI REX SCOTTORUM – John, by the grace of God, King of Scots. The Royal arms of Scotland are displayed on the shield and horse trapper, details are conventional other than the noteworthy Scottish form of the sword. (drawn by Pete Armstrong)**

RIGHT **Norhamshire formed part of the County Palatine of Durham in the middle ages. The imposing ruins of Norham Castle, the 12th century stronghold of the bishops of Durham stand guard above a crossing of the River Tweed on the Anglo-Scottish border. (Keith Durham)**

gathering ominously nearby the Scots caved in and effectively put the country under his control. It is not clear at what stage in these events he decided on the subjugation of Scotland though it is possible that unfolding circumstances simply played into his hands. Edward's beloved wife Eleanor died in 1290 and the cast of the ageing king's mind darkened. The fall of Acre in 1291 ended Edward's dream of a new crusade in the Holy Land and without this distraction his thoughts returned increasingly to Scottish affairs.

King John Balliol

The foremost of the 14 claimants to the throne were both descendants of the daughters of William the Lion's brother, David, Earl of Huntingdon. They were the octogenarian Robert Bruce known as the 'Competitor' (grandfather of King Robert I) and John Balliol. Balliol was a cultured, middle-aged Anglo-Norman nobleman with extensive estates in England, northern France and Galloway and though he had some support among the nobility of Scotland he was not generally well-known there. On 17 November 1292, at Berwick, Edward decided in favour of the claims of Balliol who rendered homage to him for his kingdom and was crowned at Scone later that month. Though Scotland's castles were nominally returned to King John the country still remained effectively under English occupation. Edward was determined to further demonstrate his dominance of Scotland by undermining the judicial independence of the kingdom. He demanded that Balliol appear in person in England to answer appeals against the judgements of the Scottish courts. In medieval law this prerogative of the overlord was held to be the very test of sovereignty. In this manner he sought to emphasise that Balliol, as his feudal vassal held his kingdom from the King of England, his overlord. Balliol was summoned to Westminster to answer an appeal by Macduff of Fife against a judgement imposed on him by the Scottish Parliament and though he refused to answer MacDuff's appeal, 'without consulting the people of his realm', the affair was a humiliation and diminished his authority with the Scottish magnates. In 1293 war flared up between Edward I and Philip IV of France over the sovereignty of Gascony. Edward sent a high-handed summons to his Scottish vassals, including King John and 18 Scottish lords, demanding feudal service abroad for their Scottish lands. With a newly constituted council of magnates at his back to stiffen his resolve, Balliol refused to comply. Instead he sent a deputation to Philip of France to seek his assistance. This resulted in the treaty that became known as 'The Auld Alliance' and provided for a Scottish invasion of England if the English invaded France. Early in 1296 Balliol formally renounced his allegiance to the English king and war between England and Scotland became inevitable. John Balliol, who a contemporary chronicler described as 'a lamb amongst wolves, who dared not open his mouth', found himself at the head of a Scotland for once united in its determination to oppose the will of Edward Plantagenet.

The proud remains of the castle of the Balliols, high above the River Tees, still dominate the old town of Barnard Castle in Co. Durham. (author's photo)

In 1296 Edward was 57 years of age and increasingly embittered by the recent Welsh rebellion and the turn of events on the continent, yet his energy was undiminished. It is a measure of the military strength of Edward I's England that the king was able to prosecute his war in Gascony against Philip of France, and at the same time assemble at Newcastle-upon-Tyne a formidable force for the invasion of Scotland. Meanwhile, aware of the threat, the Scottish feudal host assembled at Caddonlee, the traditional muster point of Scottish armies, near Selkirk. Not all Scots obeyed the summons to arms for the interests of many in the south of Scotland, prominent among whom was Patrick, Earl of Dunbar, were best served by loyalty to Edward. Nor were the Bruces in arms against the English at this time for they owed no allegiance to John Balliol. They honoured their oath of fealty to Edward I at the castle of Wark on Tweed at Easter, 1296. We have no direct evidence of the whereabouts of William Wallace at this time though it is probable that he, unlike Robert Bruce, answered the call to arms at Caddonlee. King John was not at Caddonlee, he had effectively been sidelined. Instead of him the leader of the Scots was John Comyn, Earl of Buchan, together with the earls of Menteith, Strathearn, Lennox, Ross, Atholl, Mar and John 'the red' Comyn of Badenoch. The Scots crossed the Solway into England, leaving a swathe of

In April 1296 Scottish raiders damaged the Augustinian Priory at Lanercost in Cumberland. The outraged chronicler of Lanercost responded with a lurid catalogue of Scottish atrocities against, 'infirm people, old women, women in child-bed and even children...they raised aloft little span-long children pierced on pikes...proving themselves apt scholars in atrocity.' (author's photo)

A shattered fang of masonry high above the picturesque old harbour of Dunbar in East Lothian is all that remains now to remind us of the once mighty stronghold of Patrick, Earl of Dunbar. (author's photo)

devastation in their wake. The chronicler of nearby Lanercost Priory wrote, 'burning houses, slaughtering men and driving off cattle and on the two following days they violently assaulted the city of Carlisle but failing in their attempt, they retired on the third day'. In early April the Scots raided Northumberland and Cumberland again, badly damaging the monastic houses at Lanercost and Hexham. The outraged chronicler of Lanercost recorded their atrocities and accused them of burning alive in Corbridge, 'about 200 little scholars who were in the school … learning their first letters and grammar, having blocked up the doors and set fire to the building'.

The fall of Berwick

The raids though damaging were futile and contributed nothing to defeating the English, nor did they divert Edward from his purpose. On 28 March he crossed the Tweed near Coldstream and advanced eastward towards Berwick upon Tweed. In 1296 Berwick was Scotland's most prosperous burgh and foremost in the country's commerce and overseas trade. On 29 March Edward summoned the town to surrender but the garrison with misplaced confidence met his overtures with derision and 'bared their breeches' contemptuously at him. The king launched an all-out assault on the town by land and sea. Although the naval operation was mistimed leading to some losses, the ferocity of the assault against the neglected timber palisades of the *enceinte* stunned the defenders. Resistance quickly collapsed and the demoralised Scots fell back into the town. A group of 30 Flemish merchants held out for a time in the fortified Red Hall before the building was set alight, making an end of all inside. A crossbow bolt shot by one of the Flemings killed Edward's young cousin Richard of Cornwall as he lifted his visor for air. He seems to have been the only English casualty of note at Berwick and it may have been his

ABOVE **The valley of the Spott Burn, where John de Warenne, Earl of Surrey inflicted a disastrous defeat on the Scots, is now a haven of tranquility nestling in a rural backwater of unspoiled East Lothian. (author's photo)**

ABOVE, RIGHT **The site of the battle of Dunbar, on the Spott Burn, is marked on Ordnance Survey sheet 67. The burn runs behind the wall in the foreground, right to left; the Scots were positioned on the heights above. (author's photo)**

death that sparked the king's anger, which was 'like that of a wild boar pursued by dogs'. Though the garrison of the castle, which had obligingly surrendered, and the women and children of the town were allowed to depart, the burghers and townsmen paid dearly for their earlier insults to the king for he unleashed his troops to sack the town and a bloodbath ensued, that remains a stain on the great king's reputation to this day.

The battle of Dunbar

Edward remained in Berwick for four weeks renewing and improving the defences as he intended the town to remain an English possession and to become the administrative centre of conquered Scotland. Edward appointed Hugh Cressingham as Treasurer of Scotland, with his headquarters in the town, which was soon largely repopulated with English merchants and townsmen. The Earl of Dunbar was at this time with King Edward in Berwick but his wife, who did not share his enthusiasm for the English, took the opportunity presented by the earl's absence to open the gates of the castle of Dunbar to the Scots. John de Warenne, the Earl of Surrey was despatched to retake Dunbar with a strong detachment of infantry and men-at-arms and began a blockade of the castle. Walter of Guisborough says that Warenne's force was composed of 1,000 horse exclusive of another 100 of the Bishop of Durham's cavalry and 10,000 foot, though this seems more likely to be the strength of the whole English army rather than the force detached under Warenne at Dunbar which was more likely to be the vanguard of the army. On April 27 Warenne was attacked by the main body of King John's army, the 'Feudal host of Scotland', in the expectation of trapping the earl between the main Scottish army and the castle garrison. As the Scottish host came

John Balliol was the last king of Scots to be crowned on the Stone of Destiny on the Moot Hill at Scone before Edward I took it to Westminster Abbey in 1296. It was returned to Scotland after 700 years in 1996 and is now in St Margaret's Chapel in Edinburgh Castle. Scone has to be content with a replica nowadays. (author's photo)

into view on the hills above Spott, overlooking Dunbar, Warenne left a force under Humfrey de Bohun to contain the castle garrison and turned to confront them. As the English troops deployed to cross the Spott Burn the swell of the hillside masked their advance from the Scots above who thought they were retiring. Displaying their inexperience and military ineptitude the Scots left the safety of the high ground, broke ranks and rushed headlong to defeat. Warenne's experienced troops, many of them hardened in the Welsh campaigns, cut a bloody swathe through the disordered Scots and Buchan's army disintegrated. Many of the foot were cut down but among the leaders and knights only the Sheriff of Stirling, Sir Patrick Graham, was killed during the brief melee before the Scots surrendered. The battle of Dunbar is notable for the large number of nobles and knights taken prisoner and for the devastating demonstration of the utter ineffectiveness of the Scottish military machine. There were 171 captives, earls, knights and squires. The more eminent were sent to the Tower of London, the rest were distributed to imprisonment in English castles in the midlands and south. Andrew Murray, who, in company with Wallace, was soon to rise so meteorically to fame was still only an esquire when he was taken. He was sent to Chester Castle, of the castles used to house the prisoners of Dunbar the one closest to the border.

Submission of the Scots

The backbone of Scottish resistance was broken at Dunbar. There was little fight left in them and the remaining castles still in Scottish hands were handed over one after another. At mighty Stirling the garrison fled without a fight, leaving the porter to hand over the keys. The campaign had become a military promenade and Edward progressed leisurely north through what was now, effectively, his kingdom of Scotland. John Balliol surrendered his kingdom on 10 July at Brechin and as a final indignity Edward tore the Royal Arms from his surcoat before

Ancient yew trees stand guard over the Moot Hill at Scone in Perthshire where, from time immemorial, the kings of Scots were crowned. The chapel now on the site post-dates the campaigns of Stirling bridge and Falkirk by several centuries. (author's photo)

despatching him to imprisonment in the Tower of London, 'Tuyme Tabart he was callit eftirwart'. Thus Balliol, a scapegoat for the failure of the nation, became lodged in the Scottish consciousness as 'Toom Tabard' (empty coat). As he had humiliated Balliol, Edward now sought to humiliate the Scottish nation by stripping it of the symbols of its status as an independent kingdom. He took the Scottish records and the sacred Black Rood south with him. The Stone of Destiny, on which the kings of Scotland had been crowned from time immemorial at Scone, was sent to Westminster Abbey where a wooden coronation chair was built around it. Bruce of Annandale (the ineffectual father of the Robert Bruce of Bannockburn fame) thought that his loyalty to the king would be rewarded with the crown of Scotland but his hopes were crushed by Edward's scathing retort, 'Have we nothing else to do but win kingdoms for you?' Clearly, there was to be no king in Scotland other than Edward Plantagenet. He summoned all the landholders of Scotland to Berwick to give or renew their oath of allegiance to him. The document recording their names has become known as the 'Ragman Roll'. William Wallace's name is not included and his absence from the roll has come to symbolise his independent spirit for he owed no allegiance to Edward Plantagenet, his loyalty was to Scotland.

On 17 September 1296 Edward crossed the Border, dismissing his northern conquest with a famously contemptuous remark to his old friend the Earl of Surrey, 'Bon besoigne fait qy de merde delivrer', or, in modern parlance, 'It's a relief to be rid of shit'. The king rode south and the ageing earl retired to the comfort of his estates in Yorkshire, leaving the government of a well-garrisoned Scotland in the capable hands of William Ormsby the chief justice and the rapacious treasurer Hugh Cressingham.

CHRONOLOGY

1286

18/19 March Accidental death of Alexander III of Scotland.
28 April Election of Guardians of the Realm to rule Scotland.

1290

18 July Treaty of Birgham.
26 September Death of Margaret, the 'Maid of Norway' in Orkney.
Death of Eleanor of Castile, Edward I's Queen.
Competitors for the Scottish throne dispute the succession.
Bishop Fraser writes to ask Edward to intervene in the crisis.

1291

May Edward I at Norham where an Anglo-Scottish Parliament convenes.
Edward demands to be recognised as overlord of Scotland. Edward
arbitrates between the Competitors who agree to place Scottish royal
castles in his hands, in effect putting him in possession of the kingdom.
13 June Guardians and Scots lords acknowledge Edward I as overlord
of Scotland.

1292

17 November Edward decides in favour of John Balliol.
30 November Balliol crowned King of Scots at Scone.

1295

Franco-Scottish Treaty – 'The Auld Alliance'.

1296

March War between Edward I and Scots.
30 March Sack of Berwick.
27 April Battle of Dunbar, Scots defeated.
July King John submits and resigns his kingdom to Edward I.
28 August Berwick parliament, Edward receives homage and fealty
from some 2,000 Scots; the 'Ragman Roll'.
17 September Edward I leaves Scotland, hands over the government
to John de Warenne, Earl of Surrey.

1297

May Wallace murders William Heselrig the sheriff of Clydesdale at Lanark.
Wallace raids Scone with William Douglas.
Spring/Summer Andrew Murray leads the north rising.
June–July Percy and Clifford force capitulation of Scots lords at Irvine.
22 August Edward I sails with his army for Flanders.
September Wallace and Murray join forces at the siege of Dundee.
11 September Battle of Stirling Bridge.
18 October Wallace raids Northumberland and Cumberland.
November Death of Andrew Murray.

1298

January Scots capture Stirling Castle.
Wallace knighted and elected as Guardian of Scotland.
14 March Edward returns from Flanders.
22 July Battle of Falkirk, Wallace defeated.

1299

Autumn Wallace goes abroad, Scots take Stirling Castle.

1300

July–August Edward I campaigns in Galloway.

1301

July–September Edward I and Edward of Caernarvon campaign in
southern Scotland.

1302

Truce for nine months

1303

24 February Battle of Roslin, Segrave defeated.
May Edward I invades Scotland.

1304

Submission of Comyn and other Scots lords to Edward I.
22 April Siege of Stirling Castle begins.

1305

3 August William Wallace captured near Glasgow.
23 August Wallace executed.

1306

10 February Bruce murders John, 'the red' Comyn at
Dumfries.
25 March Bruce crowned as King of Scots at Scone.
19 June Battle of Methven, Bruce defeated.
September Bruce flees to Rathlin Island.

1307

February Bruce returns to Carrick.
7 July Edward I dies at Burgh by Sands on the Solway.

OPPOSING COMMANDERS

ENGLISH COMMANDERS

Edward Plantagenet, b.1239, King Edward I, 1272–1307 (d. aged 67). Though some would dispute Edward's claim to be a truly 'great' king, he was undoubtedly the most formidable of England's medieval warrior monarchs. It was said of him that 'he was a lion for pride and ferocity, but a pard for inconstancy and changeableness, not keeping his word or promise but excusing himself with fair words'.

Edward was the eldest son of Henry III of whom it was said, 'he was a better judge of sculpture and painting than he was of men.' He was however a model of domestic virtue and ensured for his son the disciplined education of a 13th-century prince and though Edward absorbed the cultured tastes of the court he inclined towards more knightly and sporting pastimes. At the age of 15 he went to Spain to marry Eleanor of Castile. It was a political alliance to ensure the security of Gascony, last remnant of the once great Angevin Empire on the continent, but it turned out to be one of history's great love-matches. Edward spent the year after his marriage in Gascony, though still under the king's supervision, attending to administrative matters in the troublesome duchy; clearly Henry did not neglect to tutor the young Prince for kingship. On his return to England, Edward had his first experience of the realities of campaigning; in Wales, against the troublesome Llewelyn, though he met with little success. Henry III's confrontation with Simon de Montfort and the baronial party over his misgovernment led to open warfare and at Lewes in 1264, Edward had his first taste of battle. He led the royal vanguard in a headlong charge against de Montfort's left wing, which broke in rout, then incautiously pursued it far from the battlefield. By the time the ill-disciplined knights of Edward's division returned on their blown chargers the battle was lost and both the king and his son were made prisoner. The prince escaped his captors in May 1265 and revived the royal cause with the support of the lords of the Welsh marches. Between May and August 1265, in a brilliant campaign that culminated in the defeat and death of Simon de Montfort at Evesham, Prince Edward demonstrated that he had absorbed the lessons of the disaster at Lewes. In 1270 he sailed for the Holy Land with about 1,000 men, too few to reverse the decline of the Frankish states in Palestine. His 16-month campaign achieved little but added greatly to his military experience and boosted his international prestige and reputation. Henry III died in 1272, while Edward was still abroad; on his return in 1274 he was crowned in Westminster Abbey aged 35 at the height of his powers, admired and respected at home and abroad. The chronicler Nicholas Trivet described him as handsome and tall, standing head and shoulders above the common crowd (he was 6ft 2in. tall). His

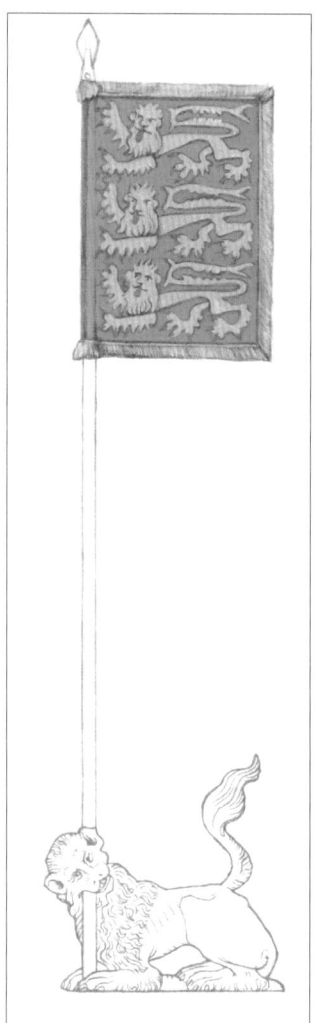

Banner of King Edward I (drawn by Pete Armstrong)

hair was black in manhood but when he grew older it became as white as a swan. His features were slightly marred by a drooping eyelid. In spite of a lisp, he was persuasive and ready in speech. His long arms made him a swordsman second to none and his long shanks gave him mastery over the most spirited stallion. When he was not fighting, his passions were hawking and the chase. He had a violent temper but was quick to forgive. The troubadours called him the best lance in all the world, possessing all the virtues of the knightly class. There were darker tales current too that suggested a vicious and vindictive side to his nature, a side that would emerge to sour the deeds of his later years.

John de Warenne, Earl of Surrey, (c.1239–1304) was a close contemporary of Edward Plantagenet to whom he was related both by his descent from Geoffrey of Anjou and by his marriage to a half-sister of Henry III. He was a companion of Prince Edward in Gascony and from an early age he shared the same education and training in knightly virtues. He fought in Prince Edward's wing at the battle of Lewes in 1264 and the following year was again with the prince when Simon de Montfort was defeated and killed at Evesham. He was one of Edward's chief commanders throughout the arduous Welsh campaigns from 1277 to 1295 and was granted lands that made him one of the most powerful of the marcher lords. In 1296 the Earl of Surrey defeated the Scots at Dunbar with only the vanguard of the English army. Some said he won by default as a result of the inept performance of the Scots rather than displaying any great tactical ability himself. It was to prove the high water mark of a long and undistinguished military career. Left to his own devices to face Wallace at Stirling Bridge he was humiliatingly defeated, yet he retained enough of the king's confidence to be given a command the following year at Falkirk. The earl had four bannerets with him at Stirling Bridge; apart from Cressingham they were all experienced professional soldiers but were unable to rectify Warenne's mistakes.

Hugh Cressingham, Treasurer of Scotland, dubbed the 'tracherer' by the Scots with whom he was not popular. Nor was he held in high esteem by the chronicler Walter of Guisborough who described him as unreliable, slippery, haughty, arrogant and avaricious. Cressingham had risen by his own efforts in the king's service and in 1297 he effectively controlled the English administration of Scotland as the Earl of Surrey, the king's lieutenant, so disliked the country that he had retired to his estates in Yorkshire. Cressingham had a large income from the parish of Rudby in Yorkshire along with other church prebends and had grown obese on the rich lifestyle they provided. He was not however without military experience as there is a record of his service in Wales during the last uprising.

Walter Huntercombe (d.1320), was an experienced officer who served Edward I throughout the Welsh and Scottish Wars. He was first summoned for service against Prince Llewelyn in 1277 and thereafter his name appears frequently in the records as a professional soldier raising and leading troops until 1310. He was in the Earl of Surrey's retinue at Stirling Bridge and had with him 32 knights and troopers. He fought at Falkirk in the division of the Bishop of Durham with 30 horse.

Profiles of King Edward I, drawn by a clerk to enliven an Exchequer Memorandum Roll, dating from 1297–98. These drawings are the nearest thing to a contemporary portrait of Edward that we have. (re-drawn by the author)

Great Seal of John de Warenne, Earl of Surrey. S'IOH'IS:DE WARENNIA:COMIT(IS)DE:SURREIA. Both the arms of Warenne and those of the Scottish Stewarts derive from those of Vermandois, 'chequy or and azure.' The seal is affixed to the baron's letter to the Pope of 1300 and may have been in use for some time as it shows the earl armed entirely in mail without any plate armour other than his outdated flat-topped helm. (author's drawing)

The rich parish of Rudby-in-Cleveland belonged to Hugh Cressingham in 1297. In an alcove in the church is the effigy of a priest, his head resting on a foliated cross and dating from about this time. Could this be Cressingham? (author's photo)

Marmaduke de Thweng of Kilton Castle in Cleveland, d.1323, 'the hero of Stirling Bridge', was a well-known professional soldier who saw much service against the Scots. He fought at Bannockburn in 1314.

William Latimer of Corby, (d.1304), was a professional soldier whose name appears frequently in the records of the Welsh and Scottish wars. He fought at Falkirk in the king's division.

Brigade Commanders at the Battle of Falkirk

The flower of the chivalry of England accompanied Edward I on his Falkirk campaign and the names of the earls and bannerets with the army are recorded by the contemporary Falkirk Roll. Their names also occur regularly in the records of Edward's almost continuous wars in Wales and on the continent.

Henry de Lacy, Earl of Lincoln, commanded the vanguard or first brigade. With him were; Humfrey de Bohun, Earl of Hereford and Constable of England; Roger Bigod, Earl of Norfolk and Earl Marshal of England, together with 18 bannerets.

Anthony Bek, Bishop of Durham, commanded the second brigade. He was engaged continuously in the service of Edward I as a counsellor, secretary and ambassador. He was as much a lay prince as priest or bishop and served the king with his knightly retinue in person. He had two earls and 24 bannerets with him.

King Edward I himself led the third brigade, a larger force than the other three divisions of the army, with two earls and 43 bannerets under his command.

John de Warenne, Earl of Surrey, commanded the fourth brigade, despite his failure at Stirling Bridge. There were three earls and 15 bannerets in his command.

SCOTTISH COMMANDERS

John Balliol of Barnard Castle, King of Scots (1292–1306), Lord of Galloway, (b.1229? d.1314). Balliol said on his expulsion from Scotland in 1296 that he had met there only 'malice, deceit, treachery and treason' and that he did not intend to 'go into the realm of Scotland at any time to come'. Nor did he, yet the Scots treated him as king *in absentia* and fought and died at Stirling Bridge and Falkirk in his name.

William Wallace, Guardian of Scotland, (Guardian from March 1298 to July 1298. b.circa1272, d.1305). Despite William Wallace's prominence as a national hero, historically he is a shadowy figure, ill documented, the facts of his life overlaid with a distorting layer of legend and folklore. Much of the myth surrounding him is derived from 'Blind Harry's' rambling epic poem *The life of Sir William Wallace* written more than a century and a half after Wallace's death. Blind Harry claimed that his poem was based on a lost prose manuscript by John Blair, Wallace's chaplain, however the epic is

The arms of Walter Huntercombe, 'ermine two bars gemel gules.' (author's drawing)

marred by glaring factual errors, chronological discrepancies and impossibly heroic exploits. It is possible, at least for the early part of the poem, which has a feeling that it might be near the truth, that Harry did rely on writings lost to us now to which he added oral tradition enlivened with tales of his hero's derring-do. There is documentary evidence that William Wallace's brothers, both Malcolm, the elder, and John, who was executed in 1307, were early supporters of Robert Bruce. William is believed to have been educated by his uncles, both priests who taught him an abiding love of liberty. It has been suggested that as a younger son William was, like his uncles before him, destined for the priesthood. Whatever path he followed in his early years, his metamorphosis into the role of rebel leader in 1297 was sparked, according to Harry, by the murder of his wife or mistress, Marion Braidfute the heiress of Lamington, by William Heselrig, the villainous sheriff of Clydesdale. Harry's tale may not ring true in every detail but it provides the motive for Wallace's transformation and for his savage slaying of Heselrig.

Wallace or 'le Waleis' means a Welshman and it is believed that William Wallace's ancestor Richard Wallace came to Scotland in the 1130s in the service of Walter Fitzalan who had been appointed as steward of the household of King David I. The Fitzalans later became the hereditary High Stewards of Scotland and ultimately the Royal House of Stewart. The Wallace family were one of the knightly families that made up the Stewart's feudal following, which allowed them such social standing as they possessed. The lands they held were in Ayrshire and later in Renfrewshire, at the very heart of the great Stewart feudal fief. It is probable that William Wallace was born at Elderslie, near Paisley in Renfrewshire though there are arguments in favour of an Ayrshire birthplace. The year of his birth has not been satisfactorily established and we can only speculate that the details of his life point to him being in the prime of life when he came to prominence in May 1297. There survives no reliable contemporary account of Wallace's appearance though traditional accounts agree that he was tall, imposingly built, standing out far above the crowd and every inch a fighting man. This may be a true reflection of Wallace for it was an era that looked for strength, military prowess and courage in its leaders, all attributes amply demonstrated by Wallace's implacable foe Edward I of England. It was also an era that looked for social status in its leaders and though Wallace's feudal relationship with the Stewarts would have been of value, he ultimately owed his prominence to his own ability for he was one of those rare immortals who tower head and shoulders above their contemporaries. There is no documentary evidence of Wallace's career before 1297, however his skilful conduct of military affairs in 1297–98 has led to suggestions that he may have had military experience before that date. As a younger, landless son it would not have been unusual if he had sought employment as a soldier, particularly, as later events were to show, as he was so well-equipped for the role. If this is so then he may have fought in Wales or on the continent in the armies of Edward I. It has been suggested that before 1297 Wallace was in fact an outlaw, a sort of Scottish Robin Hood and that he learned something of the profession of arms while living the outlaw life. Lanercost calls him 'a certain bloody man … who had been chief of brigands in Scotland.' The only documentary evidence we have is tantalisingly inconclusive, though it is possible that it does indeed provide a glimpse of Wallace's early life; it suggests a wayward

Seal of William Latimer, 'gules a cross patonce or'.
(author's drawing)

Blind Harry's *Wallace*, a rambling verse epic in impenetrable old Scots was originally written down in the 1470s and first printed in 1508. William Hamilton of Gilbertfield's version made Harry accessible to modern readers and, since its appearance in the early 18th century it has been outsold in Scotland only by the Bible. (author's photo)

ABOVE **In 1814 the first monument to Wallace in Scotland, a 21ft sandstone giant, was erected at Dryburgh by the Earl of Buchan. The sculptor John Smith carved the figure, which he surprisingly painted white. From his lofty plinth, high above the valley of the River Tweed, the Guardian glowers menacingly towards England. (author's photo)**

ABOVE, RIGHT **Cambuskenneth Abbey from which the nearby Abbey Craig, on which the National Wallace Memorial now stands, takes its name. As a youth Wallace may have accompanied his uncle, who was the priest at Dunipace, a dependency of the Abbey, on his regular visits to the mother church. (author's photo)**

and less than romantic hero. The evidence, in the form of a court document, tells us that in August 1296 a certain disreputable cleric, Matthew of York, was found guilty 'in company of a thief, one William le Waleys' of entering the house of Christina of Perth in that town and robbing her of her goods, chattels and beer to the value of 3s. There remains the possibility that Wallace's undoubted grasp of military matters was simply the product of his innate intelligence, for whatever his experience before 1297 it can hardly have prepared him for the command of an army in battle, still less for the role of Guardian of Scotland.

Andrew de Moray/Murray (d.1297). Andrew Murray was the son of Andrew Murray of Petty, Justiciar of Scotia (Scotland north of the Forth), and thus a member of the upper ranks of the knightly classes. He fought as an esquire at Dunbar where he was captured and subsequently sent into captivity at Chester Castle where he must have had time to reflect on the disaster and the need to rethink Scottish tactics and military strategy. He escaped and raised the standard of revolt in the north. It has been suggested that he was a greater moving force in the rebellion than Wallace, however his career was cut short as he died from wounds sustained at Stirling Bridge shortly after the battle. His right to an equal share of Wallace's renown died with him and it is Wallace alone who dominates histories of the period.

After the battle of Dunbar many of the militarily discredited leaders of Scotland including the earls of Athol, Ross, Menteith and John, the younger 'red' Comyn, were held prisoner in England. They had little in the way of military expertise to contribute to Wallace's rebellion anyway. The Earl of Dunbar was not alone in remaining firmly in the English camp; many others, including the future king, Robert Bruce, Earl of Carrick gave their allegiance to Edward though, it was said, 'their hearts were elsewhere'. Support for Wallace among the upper echelons of society reflected his success or failure. Most of the earls took no part in his uprising; the stakes were high and they had too much to lose.

OPPOSING ARMIES

THE ENGLISH ARMIES OF 1297–98

The tireless ambition of Edward I meant that there was almost continuous military activity throughout his reign. The need to raise, finance, command and supply large armies and naval forces for extended campaigns was beyond the capacity of the old feudal system of military service and led to a more flexible system of paid service. By the time of the Scottish War the English army with Edward I at its head was a formidable military machine.

The English Army at Stirling Bridge

The Earl of Surrey's force was hastily raised from the counties north of the Trent and included large numbers of Welshmen, it did not approach in numbers the army that Edward I led at Falkirk. Guisborough was not alone among medieval chroniclers in having no head for numbers, his estimate of 1,000 horse and 50,000 foot for Warenne's army has to be dismissed as wild exaggeration. Cressingham, the accountant, supplied more sober figures when he wrote to the king in July from Roxburgh and said that he had mustered 300 horse and 10,000 foot. At the time of Stirling Bridge the king was in Flanders with his best troops; the records show that he had with him 822 paid cavalry and 8,500 foot; it seems odd

Contemporary illustrations of horse armour are not common yet summonses for service make it clear that both knights and troopers rode 'barded' or armoured horses. Mathew Paris drew this knight in the 1250s but there is no reason to suppose that this armour was no longer in use in the 1290s. The pattern of rings on both the knight's surcoat and the horse trapper indicate that both were armoured in a similar manner. (re-drawn by the author)

Monumental brass attributed to Sir Roger Trumpington (d.1289) at Trumpington, Cambridgeshire. The only visible plate armour supplementing Sir Roger's complete harness of mail is the helm on which his head rests and the *poleyns* that guard his knees. The latter appear to be made of *cuir-bouilli* (hardened leather) and it is probable that a *cuirrie* or cuirass of similar material, as the name suggests, is hidden beneath the surcoat. The *ailletes* have been drawn behind the shoulders, out of place, in order to display the heraldry; they would have been worn at right angles to this position. The trumpets displayed on the shield, ailletes and scabbard are a play on the surname Trumpington. The monument more probably represents Sir Giles Trumpington who was summoned to serve in Flanders in 1297 and against the Scots, 25 May 1298 so he may have been at Falkirk. (drawn by Pete Armstrong)

that Cressingham claimed to have more foot with him than the king took to Flanders. The surviving records of the infantry summoned for the Caerlaverock campaign of 1300 show that about half the foot summoned actually arrived a week late at Caerlaverock Castle early in July. The 9,093 troops enrolled that month dwindled to 5,150 by August – an alarming rate of wastage. If Cressingham's motley array had dwindled at a comparable rate then his 10,000 men would have been a far more believable 5,500 men by September, the month of the battle. The army was short of heavy cavalry yet the Welsh foot should have been reliable enough and in sufficient numbers to deal with the Scots if handled properly.

The focus of military attention was far from Scotland in late 1297. The earls of Hereford and Norfolk had refused to serve in Flanders and were in arms outside London. A large body of knights loyal to the king had been ordered south with their retinues, ostensibly to defend the coast though in effect their presence in the area created a stand-off with the earls. With so many knights and troopers in Flanders or with the two earls or confronting them, there can have been few men available to send against Wallace. Only four prominent bannerets, apart from Warenne himself, are known to have been at Stirling Bridge. In comparison, there were 115 bannerets at Falkirk, suggesting that, though the battle of Stirling Bridge looms large in folklore, in scale it was modest.

The Royal Household

The Royal Household was a small standing force composed of bannerets, knights bachelor and troopers. All other corps, feudal or paid, were raised for service and disbanded afterwards. There were rather fewer than 50 knights of the household and about a hundred troopers in 1282 though the numbers were supplemented during the Scottish War by adding the retinues of certain professional captains such as Hugh Despenser and Robert Clifford. In battle household knights formed the king's personal escort while others fought as a unit in the ranks of the heavy cavalry.

The English Cavalry

To raise cavalry Edward I had to summon his feudal tenants to perform the military service they owed him. However, military necessity compelled him to supplement the inadequate feudal array with paid troops, thus taking a step towards substituting a paid national army for his feudal retinue. To qualify for knighthood in Edward's England an individual had to hold lands of a certain value known as a 'knight's fee', that was held with the obligation of military service. There were over 6,000 knight's fees in England in 1297 so there should have been that number of knights available for feudal service, however nothing like this number ever set out on campaign.

The feudal cavalry did not want for individual bravery but lacked discipline and organisation, and in particular a proper command structure, a state of affairs that was aggravated by the pride and arrogance of their leaders. The period of 40 days for which the feudal cavalry could be summoned to serve was outdated by the later years of Edward's reign, although there were ways in which this could be extended. In fact from the First Welsh War of 1277 the king had realised that a more efficient system was to use bodies of paid troops under professional captains that could be combined into larger coherent units. The muddled groupings of the feudal cavalry could not match the paid cavalry in effectiveness.

The cavalry was officered by knights banneret who were entitled to display a square banner and ranked above ordinary knights or knights bachelor as they were sometimes termed. Any successful soldier could earn the right to fly the square banner, though there was a prejudice in favour of those with land and money to support the rank. Below the knights in rank and accordingly mounted on less valuable horses were the esquires, who served their apprenticeship in the ranks but had the social background to aspire to knighthood, and the plain troopers who had not. Wages reflected the differences in rank, a banneret received 4 shillings a day, a knight 2 shillings and a squire or trooper 1 shilling. The quality of horses similarly varied; at one end of the scale the charger or 'destrier' that the famous Robert Clifford rode at Falkirk cost £30 while at the other end, John Wetherington, a trooper, rode a rough dapple grey nag worth only eight marks. The paid cavalry provided their own horses and armour though they were recompensed by the king for losses in war.

Mounted troops were recruited, typically, by a baron or banneret, who would raise by contract a squadron of perhaps 100 horsemen and put himself at the disposal of the king for a fee. The captain's own troop might be 30 or 40 strong, the remainder, under less prominent bannerets, as sub-contractors would be 10–15 strong and be composed of a varying proportion of knights and troopers. Several of these squadrons would be joined together to form a brigade on campaign. The paid system thus gave the king the subordination of command he needed.

Surviving rolls of the paid cavalry at Falkirk show that there were 214 bannerets and knights, 642 troopers of retinues and 258 unattached lances, a total of 1,114 lances. The feudal cavalry can be reckoned from the lists of letters of protection issued and amounted to about 1,000 lances. The strength of Edward's cavalry force at Falkirk then was between 2,100 and 2,200 lances.

The English Infantry

The feudal system was never designed to provide infantry or a transport corps or engineers; proper infantry and workmen had to be paid wages. The Statute of Winchester of 1285 formalised military obligations in England; the infantry was drawn from those holding £10 or less in land who were obliged to provide themselves with armour and weapons according to their status and all men between 16 and 60 were obliged to serve for 40 days a year. These troops were paid once they were outside their county boundaries. The procedure for raising troops was for the county sheriff to provide men from whom a Commissioner of Array, usually an experienced knight or a member of the royal household, selected the most suitable to fulfil the required quota. They were organised into companies of 100 men under a mounted officer or *centenar* who was paid 1 shilling a day. The companies were divided into sections of 19 men

The knight's flowing surcoat contrasts with the stiffness of the horse-covering showing that some form of fairly rigid horse armour or 'barding' is indicated. (re-drawn after M. Paris by the author)

Only the better-off knights would have been able to afford a mail bard such as this to protect their costly destriers. A roll of 1277 notes; 16 shillings paid for 'linen coverings to put under the mail to prevent it galling the horse.' (late-13th century drawing, re-drawn by the author)

A continental illustration of the early 13th century shows a form of padded and quilted horse-armour, suggested by the way the coverings of the two armoured horses have been drawn. (re-drawn by the author)

who were paid 2d a day under *vintenars* or 'twentieth men', paid at 4d. By 1298 the infantry were beginning to be regimented into *millenaries* or units of 1,000, commanded by a *millenar*, though still subdivided into companies as before. There is documentary evidence from Edward I's time that the infantry were issued with cloth arm-pieces marked with the cross of St George.

Edward's best troops at this time were drawn from Wales and the marcher counties bordering Wales, where the recent wars had bred a race of hardy fighters. The men of northern England were reliable in defence of their home counties but were unwilling to serve in Scotland as their proximity to the Border left them open to Scottish retaliation. Edward's armies were strong in engineers and artillerymen though they found little outlet for their talents in Scotland before the siege of Stirling in 1303

Longbowmen

The chronicler Gerald of Wales noted that there was a characteristic difference between Welshmen; those of the north fought as spearmen while the men of the south were longbowmen. Gerald describes the archers of Gwent, with their 'bows of wild elm, unpolished, rude and uncouth' and tells of the great range and power of their weapons. It had been demonstrated on a small scale during the Welsh Wars that longbowmen, skilfully deployed in combination with the cavalry, could turn the tide of battle. The effectiveness of this tactical combination was underlined by Edward I on the grand scale at Falkirk. In the last decade of the 13th century military archery was still a predominantly Welsh preserve and Walter of Guisborough could still assert that at Falkirk almost all the archers were Welsh. Yet in a mere 30 years, by the early days of Edward III, the reputation of English archers was to eclipse that of the Welsh and the bow had become the English weapon *par excellence*.

Early in 1298 Edward assembled an astonishing 21,500 foot at Newcastle. This was the largest Edwardian army raised, yet it was nevertheless feeble and unwieldy. The raw troops were little more than a rabble and were quickly disbanded to be replaced by more reliable men. On his return from Flanders in March of that year Edward summoned 10,500 infantry from Wales and the Welsh marches and 2,000 more from Cheshire and Lancashire which should have given the king 12,500 infantry for the campaign that was to culminate at Falkirk. Clearly Edward did not take the threat of Wallace lightly as this is a larger force of infantry than he took to Flanders to confront the French. There is no way of knowing what proportion of spearmen there were to archers as the records do not mention the weapons of the foot, though Guisborough says that in Flanders the French dared not attack Edward because of the number of archers he had with him, which points to a formidable array of bowmen.

The seal of Roger, Count of Foy, c.1241. The knight is difficult to interpret but the horse seems to be covered by a quilted form of armour. (re-drawn by the author)

Crossbowmen

Crossbowmen were organised as a separate corps and were paid 4d a day and their vintenars 6d, wages in line with those of skilled craftsmen. They were held in high repute and had a superior status to mere *pedites* or foot, including longbowmen, who were paid 2d a day, the same as an unskilled labourer. Crossbows at this time were spanned with the aid of a foot stirrup and a belt hook, though mounted men may have used a goat's-foot lever. The weapon was popular with mounted troops as it could be loaded and fired from the saddle, there was no recoil and the weapon could be discharged one-handed if required. The bows themselves were of composite wood and horn construction, they were powerful weapons though slower than the longbow to load and fire. The weapon was never popular in England and was fast being replaced in Edward's field armies by the longbow. Professional crossbowmen were employed in small units of ten or 15 in the garrisons of Edward's newly acquired Scottish castles. Early in 1298 there were 250 foot crossbowmen with John de Warenne, Earl of Surrey, in Northumberland. If these remained in pay and were combined with Edward's Gascon corps which included 100 mounted crossbowmen there could have been about 500 men armed with this weapon at Falkirk.

Knight's war-saddle of the mid-13th century, from an English source. (author's drawing)

THE SCOTTISH ARMY OF 1297–98

Since the battle of Largs in 1263 Scotland had been at peace, and consequently her military institutions had stagnated and her leaders had little experience of the realities of war. In 1296 the Scottish 'host' was summoned for 'free service' from the free men of Scotland, the landholding and propertied classes alone. This force, which was predominantly made up of the nations feudal cavalry, demonstrated its inadequacy at the battle of Dunbar.

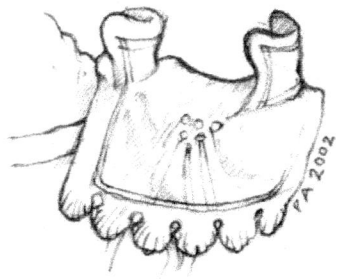

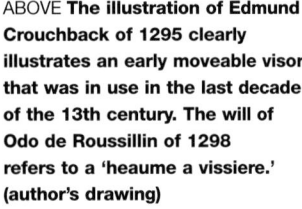

ABOVE **The illustration of Edmund Crouchback of 1295 clearly illustrates an early moveable visor that was in use in the last decade of the 13th century. The will of Odo de Roussillin of 1298 refers to a 'heaume a vissiere.' (author's drawing)**

ABOVE, RIGHT **The drawings in the initial letter of the Carlisle Charter of 1316 are the only illustrations of Scottish troops of this time. There are six of them, two bowmen, a miner, a spearman, an axeman and an artilleryman about to release the firing mechanism of a trebuchet with his mallet. Two Scots carry shields, both of triangular 'heater' form; the bows, axes and spears shown are of conventional type. They may be wearing an early form of the 'plaid', drawn up over the head as protection against the weather which was memorably bad at the time of the siege of Carlisle. The artilleryman has an open-faced helmet or** *bascinet*, **the other Scots seem to have some sort of head protection similar in shape to that of the soldier above in the turret. The drawing of the miner displays this better than the others. (author's drawing)**

The army that Wallace and Murray called out the following year was raised on the basis of 'Scottish service' which was distinct from 'free service' in that it applied to all the land and to all adult males from the 'horseless classes', which meant those who would serve as infantry. They were required to have appropriate arms and armour and an inspection or 'wapinshaw' was carried out regularly to ensure their efficiency. Every territorial unit in Scotland was obliged to provide a certain number of fighting-men, it was something like the Anglo-Saxon 'fyrd'. Organisation was on a provincial basis, the men of a particular region would turn out under their local lords as the army of the province or earldom. By calling on the population for 'Scottish service', Andrew Murray and William Wallace raised the common army of the realm and, after Stirling Bridge, titled themselves 'commanders of the army of Scotland'. The earls gave their tacit approval to the summons of the armies of their earldoms in defence of the realm but stayed at home themselves. Substantial numbers of the commonalty of the country responded with popular enthusiasm to the call to arms.

The Scottish Infantry

Before Stirling Bridge both Wallace and Murray commanded highly mobile strike forces, essentially raiders composed of a few hundred men, mounted on nags and ponies. They were mounted infantry rather than a cavalry force as they rode to the scene of action then dismounted to fight on foot. Medieval Scottish armies were essentially made up of lowland infantry and the majority were armed with 'natures weapon', the long 12 or 14ft spear or pike. They were organised into large operational formations or 'schiltrons' for battle. If the *Scotichronicon* of Walter Bower, a later source, is to be relied on there was a command structure within these formations essentially similar to that employed by the English. According to Bower a *quaternion* had

The Scottish national flag and arms, 'azure a saltire argent' are of great antiquity and it is likely that the Scottish infantry wore this badge from an early date. (author's drawing)

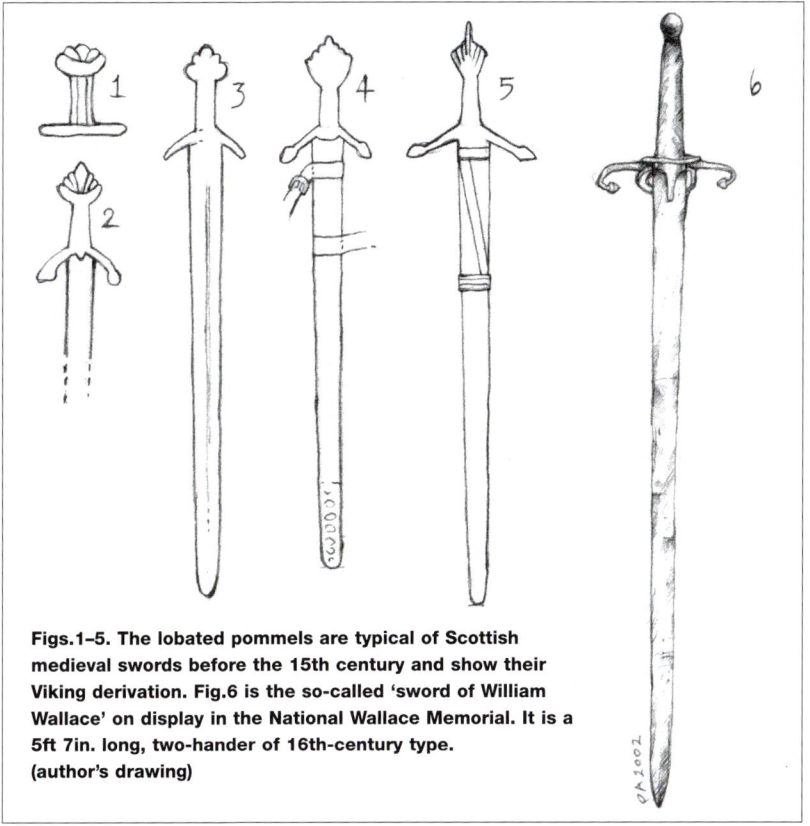

Figs.1–5. The lobated pommels are typical of Scottish medieval swords before the 15th century and show their Viking derivation. Fig.6 is the so-called 'sword of William Wallace' on display in the National Wallace Memorial. It is a 5ft 7in. long, two-hander of 16th-century type. (author's drawing)

four men under him, the smallest unit, and two quaternions were commanded by a *decurion*. There were company commanders with 100 men and regimental sized units of 1,000 men under a *chiliarch*. If this was so, and we can hardly doubt that there was a subordination of command within the Scottish army, then the Scots were no less well organised than the English. The system was not an innovation of Wallace's, the structure was already in place in 1297. His contribution was to use the existing structure to train and field an army capable of opposing the might of Edward I who he knew would march north the following year.

The Schiltron

The term 'schiltron' is used by Walter of Guisborough to describe the formations of Scottish spearmen at Falkirk, '…the circles of footmen, which circles are called schiltrouns.' Later uses of the term by other writers imply that no particular formation is meant other than the men being in close order. The term translates as 'shield wall' but we can't be sure that the spearmen actually carried shields or targes. It seems unlikely as in battle formation they would have had to sling them on their backs as the long, unwieldy spears were wielded with both hands. The schiltrons were probably formed six ranks deep with the better-armoured men in the front ranks. Wallace's schiltrons fought a defensive battle at Falkirk and this has led to their ability to manoeuvre being questioned. Yet at Stirling Bridge, far from standing on the defensive, the Scots who were presumably aligned in close order, that is to say in a schiltron or series of them, attacked in style and drove the English into the river. Their formation was unlikely to have been a circle as at Falkirk yet there seems no reason to suppose that a circle of spearmen cannot manoeuvre as well as any other formation. At Falkirk, Edward simply didn't give the schiltrons the opportunity to manoeuvre.

Scottish Archers

Wallace recognised the threat posed by the English longbowmen to his schiltrons of spearmen and recruited archers probably from Ettrick Forest to support them. They were in turn armed with the longbow; the yew bowstaves for these were probably imported through the Hanseatic ports, traditional trading partners of the Scots. There is no reason to suppose that the men of Ettrick used a shorter less powerful bow than the English and Welsh as has sometimes been suggested. The tradition of archery was not strong in Scotland but the inferiority of the Scots bowmen lay in their numbers rather than in their lack of the longbow. Wallace himself was associated with the weapon, not the giant 'claymore' of tradition or fantasy, and used the bow as a device on his seal.

The Scottish Cavalry

Scotland simply did not have the resources to field a force of heavy armoured cavalry to match the mounted chivalry of England. This was amply demonstrated at the battle of Dunbar and again at Falkirk. Guisborough is unreliable when dealing with large numbers but as the numbers he speaks of decrease his plausibility increases, so when he says that Wallace had 180 cavalry at Stirling Bridge we must incline to take this seriously. The Comyns and other earls lent support, though not their presence, to Wallace at Falkirk and contributed a small cavalry force, probably numbering less than 500 horsemen. Guisborough says that they, 'fled without a stroke of the sword.' Some said there was treachery afoot but more probably the Scottish horsemen were simply swept from the field by the superior English cavalry.

THE CAMPAIGN OF 1297

REBELLION IN SCOTLAND

Only the overgrown earthworks of the castle at Lanark survive now; a brass plaque at the entrance to the bowling club, that now occupies the site, reminds visitors of its former importance. The Scalacronica contains an eyewitness account of the events at Lanark in May 1297 that tells not only of the slaying of Heselrig but of the ordeal of Thomas Gray, the author's father, who was wounded and left for dead in the fighting. He lay in the open stripped quite naked all night but luckily the heat from burning houses kept him alive until daybreak when he was discovered by his friend, William Lundy, who took him to safety. (author's photo)

Edward had not long left Scotland before resentment of English domination revealed itself in local disturbances and early in 1297 this flared into widespread open revolt. The conquest of Scotland had been too easy and the occupation was too superficial, the Scots were not ready to resign themselves to foreign domination and Edward's Scottish empire began to crumble. The English blamed Robert Wishart, Bishop of Glasgow and James the Stewart as the instigators of the rebellion and with some justification. The Church of Scotland was resentful at Edward's appointment of English priests to Scottish benefices and had an ideal network for disseminating inflammatory ideas and justifying violence against the English. The chronicle of Lanercost believed that 'evil priests are the cause of the people's ruin, so the ruin of the realm of Scotland had its source within the bosom of her own Church.' James the Stewart and Wishart were clearly closely involved with Wallace, in fact Lanercost thought that they plotted the revolt and encouraged Wallace to the open violence which they dared not resort to themselves. At the outset of the rebellion the Stewart was one of the few Scottish lords to play a prominent role, later, as the outcome became more doubtful, in common with the other Scottish magnates his support was tempered by a more ambiguous

Scarp of motte   Moat   Top of motte-hill

Natural ditch or gully

THE CAMPAIGN OF 1297

1. May 1297: Wallace murders the sheriff of Clydesdale.
2. May 1297: Wallace and William Douglas raid Scone.
3. June/July 1297: Scots lords capitulate to Percy and Clifford at Irvine.
4. Wallace and Murray join forces at Dundee. Alexander Scrymgeour left in charge of siege. Scots army marches south for Stirling, Sept 1297.
5. Stirling Castle left in care of Thweng and Fitzwarin but falls to Scots late 1297.
6. Wallace takes town of Berwick but the castle holds out.
7. 18 Oct–22 Nov 1297: Wallace raids north of England. His HQ is in the Forest of Rothbury.
8. Carlisle defies 'William the Conqueror', Oct 1297, he burns the surrounding countryside.
9. Clifford raids Annandale before Christmas 1297, he burns Annan.

R O S S

Avoch Castle

Inverness — Taken Aug 1297

Elgin — Taken Aug 1297

Banff — Taken Aug 1297

Early 1297: Murray fails to take Urquhart.

Urquhart Castle

Loch Ness

Spey

M O R A Y

B U C H A N

Aberdeen

1 Aug 1297: Henry de Lathom seizes castle of Aberdeen for Scots

A T H O L L

M A R

Dee

The Mounth

A N G U S

Brechin

Montrose

Aug 1297-98: Siege of Dundee

Arbroath

Argyll

② Scone

Perth

May 1297

Dundee

④

Firth of Tay

Sept 1297: Wallace & Murray from Dundee.

Loch Lomond

Forth

F I F E

11 Sept 1297

⑤ Stirling

Cambuskenneth Abbey

Loch Leven

Firth of Forth

Warenne and Cressingham, 2nd week in September.

Torwood

Falkirk

Linlithgow

Leith

Dirleton Castle

Tantallon Castle

Dunbar

Bute

Glasgow

Elderslie

Bothwell

Edinburgh

Firth of Clyde

Clyde

July 1297: Cressingham awaits Warenne.

28 July 1297: Warenne arrives in Berwick.

Arran

③ Irvine

June–July 1297

Lanark

May 1297 ①

Sept 1297: Route of English army.

Tweed

⑥ Berwick upon Tweed

Sept 1297

Ayr

Forest of Selkirk

Selkirk

Ancrum

Roxburgh

Norham

Wark

18 Oct 1297: Scots invade north of England.

Jedburgh

Teviot

N O R T H U M B E R L A N D

⑦ Alnwick

Rothbury Forest

Oct–Nov 1297

G a l l o w a y

Nithsdale

Annandale

Lochmaben

Dumfries

Liddel

Rede

Cheviot Hills

Nov 1297: Scots return north.

⑨

Annan

Nov–Dec 1297

Fords

⑧ Carlisle

Oct 1297

Lanercost Priory

Hexam

Tyne

Newcastle upon Tyne

Inglewood Forest

Eden

E N G L A N D

Cockermouth

Oct–Nov 1297

Penrith

C U M B E R L A N D

Solway Firth

Stainmore

Brough

Bowes

Barnard Castle

D U R H A M

N

Route of Scots, Oct–Nov 1297
English army
Clifford raids Annandale, Nov–Dec 1297

0   25 miles
0   25 km

30

stance. The attitude of the Scottish lords in 1297 was well summed up by Walter of Guisborough, 'The common folk of the land followed him [Wallace] as their leader and ruler; the retainers of the great lords adhered to him; and even though the lords themselves were present with the English king in body, at heart they were on the opposite side.' The lords had much to lose, they had submitted to Edward after their defeat in 1296, if they rebelled again they risked forfeiting everything.

Many ordinary Scots were aghast when Cressingham issued orders that all the wool in Scotland was to be requisitioned to be sold in Flanders to finance Edward's French war. Though it was evidently intended to eventually repay the producers, the treasurer was not trusted and many feared for their livelihoods. The same 'middling folk' whose wool had been requisitioned were alarmed by well-founded reports that Edward would conscript large numbers of them for service in his armies overseas. That these demands were made by a foreign oppressor only accentuated these grievances and provided specific motivation for a nationalistic uprising.

William Wallace 'Raises his Head'

We have no record of Wallace's exploits before May 1297 when, in the telling words of the Scottish chronicler Fordun, he 'raised his head'. In that month William Heselrig, the English Sheriff of Clydesdale, was in Lanark to preside over a session of the county court. Wallace and his band took the sheriff and his men by surprise in a daring nocturnal raid that left Heselrig and many of his men dead and the town in flames. The murder of Heselrig projected Wallace, fully fledged, into the spotlight of history and laid the foundation of his immense popular reputation; he quickly became the focus of the rebellion. The Scottish chronicler Fordun attributed the best of motives to those who joined him; 'From that time there gathered to him all who were of bitter heart and were weighed down beneath the burden of bondage under the intolerable rule of English domination and he became their leader.' Far from hiding from the wrath of the English after his exploit at Lanark, Wallace boldly raided Scone with a well-mounted force that included Sir William Douglas and his followers; his target was William Ormsby the English justiciar of Scotland. Ormsby escaped but the raid ensured that the English north of the Forth became virtually prisoners behind the walls of their own castles.

Capitulation at Irvine

Meanwhile the lords of south-west Scotland were in arms, led by the Bishop of Glasgow, Robert Wishart, James the Stewart and Robert Bruce, Earl of Carrick and king to be, who appears for the first time as a leader of resistance to the English. Edward I sent a force of northern troops under Robert Clifford, the Keeper of the Marches, and Henry Percy, Warden of Galloway, to arrest, imprison and bring to justice these disturbers of his peace. The inept Scots lords backed down and surrendered at Irvine early in July without striking a blow though the protracted negotiation of the terms of submission that followed occupied Percy and Clifford for weeks and gained time for the rebellion. The capitulation at Irvine once again humiliated and discredited the nobility, leaving Wallace as the undisputed leader of the revolt in southern and central Scotland. One Scottish knight, Richard Lundie, of whom we shall hear more, was so disgusted by the fiasco that he promptly changed sides. Bruce agreed to formally submit in Berwick but never turned up, and Wishart his guarantor was arrested and confined in Roxburgh Castle. William Douglas was kept in chains in Berwick Castle where his jailers found him savage and abusive; he was sent to the Tower of London where he died. His son James was only ten years old and would grow up to be the famous 'Good' Sir James Douglas who, as a companion of Robert Bruce, played so prominent a role in the wars of independence in the next century. Wallace showed his anger at Wishart's betrayal of the cause by raiding the bishop's palace at Ancrum, seizing his property and taking his sons captive.

The northern Rising of 1297

Early in 1297 Andrew Murray escaped from Chester Castle, where he had languished since his capture at Dunbar, and returned to the family lands in the north east of Scotland where he raised the standard of revolt. As the son of a high ranking knight Andrew Murray was a natural leader of the northern rebellion but there were others too; notably Alexander Pilche, a burgess of Inverness, who joined forces with Murray as his lieutenant. It is mainly from letters sent to Edward I from his 'diligent and faithful friends' in the north that we are able to piece together a few details of the rebellion. Their letters told the king of the rapidly deteriorating situation in the north and begged for his assistance against Murray and the 'very large body of rogues' he led. Murray's early attempt to take the English-held Castle Urquhart on the shore of Loch Ness was foiled by a spirited defence but, as the strength of his following increased, the castles of Inverness, Elgin and Banff fell to him and by early August he had practically swept the English out of Moray and the country north of the mountainous Mounth.

Robert Clifford's castle at Brough in Cumbria's Eden Valley stands sentinel above the old town. The castle was destroyed by the Scots in 1174. The stone keep we see now dates from its subsequent rebuilding. It passed to the Cliffords from the Vipoint family in the 13th century. (author's photo)

Most of the Scottish leaders, who had been in English captivity since Dunbar, were released in the summer of 1297 on condition that they serve with the king in Flanders. However when Edward became aware of the worsening situation in Scotland he ordered John Comyn of Badenoch and John Comyn, Earl of Buchan to quell the rebels instead of joining his army abroad. Their attempts to co-ordinate action against the rebellion in the north were ineffective. Cressingham was of the well-founded opinion that the loyalty of the Comyns to the English king was lukewarm, like many other Scottish lords. Cressingham's letters to the king betray his desperation as he warns that most of his officials 'have been killed, besieged or imprisoned or have abandoned their bailiwicks and dare not go back. And in some shires the Scots have appointed and established [their own] bailiffs and officials. Thus no shire is properly kept save for Berwickshire and Roxburghshire.' That this was entirely the work of Wallace of course is impossible, the community of Scotland on all levels must have co-operated to get some form of administration back in place which enabled him to gather, train and complete the equipment of his forces that July in Selkirk Forest. In August Wallace left the forest of Selkirk and turned his attention north of the Forth. He swept across Perthshire and Fife, clearing the English from these areas before laying siege to the important castle of Dundee. Andrew Murray and Wallace were in communication with each other and both leaders were aware that an English army had crossed the Border. They would have been in no doubt that the English objective was Stirling and that their intention was to settle with the rebels. Murray and his northern army marched south and met Wallace at Dundee early in September. There the two leaders of the revolt joined forces. They left the siege in the hands of the burgesses of Dundee, to be prosecuted 'on pain of loss of life and limb' and hurried south to take up a position outside Stirling.

On 22 August, the king sailed for Flanders in the cog *Edward* to resume his war against the French, his Scottish contingent amounted to a paltry ten knights and 25 squires and troopers under Edward Comyn and these slipped away and made their way home at the first opportunity.

Mighty Stirling Castle, perched high on its rock, dominating the town and the bridge over the River Forth had been in English hands since its surrender after the battle of Dunbar. It stands guardian in the narrow waist of Scotland that separates the north and south of the realm, guarded on the west by the Touch and Fintry Hills and to the east by the tidal River Forth that flows in a short distance into the Firth of Forth. The castle and bridge at Stirling were the keys to northern Scotland.

Seal of Henry Percy of Topcliff, Warden of Galloway. Henry Percy was knighted by the king at Berwick in 1296. He campaigned in Scotland or defended the Marches constantly until his death (10 October 1314) shortly after Bannockburn. At Falkirk he had five knights and two troopers in his retinue and fought in the brigade of his uncle, the Earl of Surrey. (author's drawing)

The English march north to confront the rebels

Hugh Cressingham was at Roxburgh when Percy and Clifford, returning from their success at Irvine, told him of the capitulation of the Scots lords and warned him of the threat of William Wallace on the other side of the country. It was decided that an expedition against the Scots must await the Earl of Surrey's arrival whereupon Percy and Clifford departed and presumably disbanded most of their troops. On 28 July the dilatory earl arrived in Berwick with his nephew, Henry Percy, who must have joined him after leaving Roxburgh. The earl left his nephew to await the arrival of Bruce and the rest, who were pledged to formally offer their submission in Berwick by the end of that month, and rode to join Cressingham who on 23 July had written that he had 300 horse and 10,000 foot with him at Roxburgh. The English army, reinforced by Warenne's retinue, toiled northward across the Lammermuir Hills, through Lauderdale, the shortest practical route for an army encumbered by a train of wheeled transport. There was an 'abundance of ships in Berwick should the earl make a foray…' reported Cressingham, so supplies must also have been sent up to Stirling by sea; the logistics of the campaign at least seem well contrived. Stirling was only five days march from Roxburgh yet it seems that Warenne did not arrive there until the second week in September by which time the Scots were already in a strong position north of the Forth and the campaigning season was well advanced.

THE BATTLE OF STIRLING BRIDGE

Contemporary Sources

The chronicle of Walter Hemingborough of Guisborough Priory in the Cleveland area of North Yorkshire is the key contemporary source for the battles of Stirling Bridge and Falkirk. In fact he is the main source of our knowledge of Scottish affairs at this time. Walter's chronicle is reliable and well informed; his accounts of these battles are practically all we have to go on; there are no other detailed accounts against which to check his facts. Within a short distance of Guisborough Priory stood Kilton Castle, home of Marmaduke de Thweng. The amount of ink devoted by Walter to the heroic exploits of Marmaduke at Stirling Bridge strongly suggests that he was the author's informant on this affair. Unfortunately at the time of the battle of Falkirk Marmaduke was a prisoner of the Scots so he cannot have been of use to Walter regarding the details of that battle. There is no internal evidence in Walter's account of Falkirk to suggest the source of his information though many northern knights, including men whose lands bordered those of the priory, fought there. There are persuasive indications in Walter's chronicle that he and Hugh Cressingham were well acquainted. Cressingham had connections in the Guisborough area and Walter never misses an opportunity to portray him in an unflattering light. My account of the battle follows that of Walter of Guisborough closely.

The remains of the Augustinian priory at Guisborough in North Yorkshire where the monk Walter Hemingborough wrote his famous chronicle. (author's photo)

The Terrain of the Battlefield

Medieval Stirling Bridge was a substantial wooden structure, carried on eight stone piers, though barely wide enough to allow the passage of a horse and cart. Recently traces of the masonry footings of the bridge have been discovered that show that it stood a matter of yards upstream of the 'Old Bridge', the 15th century stone structure now used as a footbridge. The surviving pier footings now span the Forth at an angle rather than crossing directly, although this may be due to the river having changed course over the centuries. The medieval bridge would have obligingly disgorged Warenne's troops into an enveloping meander of the river. They probably formed into battle order north of the loop but the siting of the loops of the river ensured that the Scottish attack would inevitably drive many of the outnumbered English back into the trap formed by the meander. From the bridge, a raised track or causeway ran north-west across soft meadowland that could turn quickly to bog after heavy rain but soon gave way to a firmer area of cultivation. Beyond this the wooded Abbey Craig, an outlier of the Ochil Hills, rises 360ft above the flat plain of the Forth. Both the Abbey Craig and Stirling Castle, perched on its rock across the river a mile and a half distant, provide a panorama of the battlefield. Just over a mile upstream as the crow flies from the bridge at Stirling, between the tidal limit and the

point where the River Teith enters the Forth, is the site of the ford that Richard Lundie said was passable 'sixty at a time.' The area today is much changed since Wallace's day by modern road building and drainage work and the river runs wide and deep making it difficult to accept Lundie's statement. Nor is it easy to accept that a ford here was ever passable all year round or after heavy rain, or that it could have presented an easy passage across the river. The ford at Drip, a little upstream beyond the confluence with the Teith, may have presented an easier crossing but the road beyond led in a north-westerly direction and Lundie's force would have had to circle north in order to ford the Teith before they were able to threaten Wallace's flank. The fords of Frew were no doubt well known and passable in 1297, but they are six miles above Stirling, too far to be Lundie's suggested crossing place.

OPENING MOVES

A prelude to the battle was provided by James the Stewart and the Earl of Lennox in company with certain other Scots lords who joined the Earl of Surrey at Stirling. They probably had little choice as, having submitted to Edward I, they would have been summoned to serve with his forces at Stirling. The motivation behind their comings and goings before the battle was almost certainly selfish; they were waiting to see how the situation developed, with a foot in both camps. The Stewart and his company suggested to the earl that, given a little time, they might be able to speak with the Scots leaders and resolve the situation peacefully. Nothing resulted from their embassy to Murray and Wallace, neither of whom would have trusted the Stewart and his companions after their climb-down at Irvine; the duplicity of the approach must have been apparent to both. The Stewart and his company returned to the English camp at Stirling on 10 September and promised to reinforce the earl's forces the following day with 40 armoured horse. As they rode off that evening they met a band of returning foragers with whom an argument broke out during which the Earl of Lennox wounded one of the footsoldiers in the neck with his sword. Word of this incident spread throughout the army and the wounded man's comrades brought him before the Earl of Surrey demanding vengeance that very night. But the earl told them to await the morning and see whether the Scots lords kept their promise; for then they would be better able to demand satisfaction for the insult. Then, leaving orders that the army was to be ready to cross the bridge in the morning, the earl retired to his bed. He was 66 years of age and ailing, he had written to the king to complain of his ill health the previous month and had expected to be replaced in Scotland by Brian Fitzalan of Bedale. However difficulties over the latter's pay had obliged the ageing earl to remain in his post and return north to a command that he viewed with some distaste. At sunrise the army began to cross the river, the bridge was only wide enough for two horsemen abreast so it took some time for the vanguard to cross, however they were recalled and re-crossed the bridge, because the earl had not yet risen. When Warenne did rise, in keeping with tradition, before battle was joined he conferred knighthood on several of the squires present, of whom, as Guisborough glumly recounts, many were to fall that day. The army then began to cross the bridge again but was again recalled, this time because the Stewart and Lennox rode into camp and the earl thought that they came with offers of a Scottish submission. He was mistaken, they had only excuses to offer, for they had neither persuaded the Scots to submit nor brought the promised 40 men-at-arms. Finally, Warenne sent two Dominican friars to treat with the Scots leaders on the Abbey Craig. But the Scots were defiant and sent the messengers back with the famous retort that Guisborough credits to Wallace; 'Take back this reply, that we are not here to make peace but to do battle to defend ourselves and liberate our kingdom. Let them come on and we shall prove this in their very beards.'

The Stage is set for battle
The army that Wallace and Murray gathered together at Stirling was more than a combination of the mobile raiding forces with which they had operated previously. Their forces were supplemented by newly arrived men, raised from the armies of the earldoms, men who were by law required to be well armed and equipped and the best of whom would have formed the front ranks of the schiltrons. The army was hastily assembled and the Scots leaders would have had only a little time to train the men to form and manoeuvre in the large formations necessary for battle, nevertheless as events were to prove, the short time available served well enough. The Scots' position in the woods about the Abbey Craig allowed them to challenge any attempt to cross the Forth and to observe the movements of the enemy while keeping their own forces concealed.

They were playing a watching and waiting game that could result in either a battle, if the situation was favourable, or a withdrawal in adverse

STIRLING BRIDGE – WILLIAM WALLACE AND ANDREW MURRAY ON THE ABBEY CRAIG (pages 38–39)

High on the Abbey Craig, William Wallace delivers his famous rejection of the English terms of submission delivered by the Dominicans sent by John de Warenne as envoys to the Scots. There would have been many such clerks and non-combatants employed in the earl's extensive household. Wallace (1), as befits his status as joint commander of the army of Scotland, is armed conventionally. His armour and weapons are products of the finest continental craftsmanship. At his side his young squires (2) carry his shield and helm. Behind the apprehensive friars (3) stands Sir Andrew Murray (4), flanked by his banner (5) and that of St Andrew (6), the ancient national flag of Scotland. The saint's cross is worn as a badge on the padded *akheton* of the well-equipped spearman in the foreground (7) and by the fighting men of the schiltrons assembled on the plain below (8). In the distance, beyond the loops of the River Forth the mighty fortress of Stirling (9) stands guard over the bridge where English troops are assembling. The arms of Andrew Murray are known from a seal attached to a document of 1296. William Wallace's arms are unknown though he is generally attributed with 'gules a lion rampant argent'. The seal attached to the so-called 'Lubeck letter', which was sent by Wallace and Murray to the citizens of that town after their victory at Stirling Bridge, survives – one of the few artefacts that have come down to us that can be connected with Wallace. It displays the Royal Arms of Scotland on the front but the reverse, which is of most interest to us, shows a hand drawing an arrow on a bow. Had this seal been Murray's it must have displayed the stars used as charges by his family. He was, by the time the letter was sent to Lubeck either dead or dying of wounds sustained in the battle, so logically this must be the seal used by Wallace. The bow and arrow device is not displayed on a shield as would be usual with a heraldic charge, so it doesn't really amount to a coat of arms as such. The faint inscription surrounding the image of the bow and arrow reads: [WILELM]VS FILIVS ALANI WALAIS, that is 'William Son of Alan Wallace', which throws new light on the name of William's father. An Alan Wallace, a crown tenant of Ayrshire, sealed the Ragman Roll in 1296 when he submitted to Edward I. There are several Ayrshire Wallace seals attached to the Ragman Roll but none of them display a lion. The devices used are a fleur de Lys, a curlew with foliage behind, and a cross paty. The attribution of a rampant lion to Wallace is probably simply due to the notion that, as Scotland herself is symbolised by the king of beasts, what could be more fitting for Scotland's National Hero? (Angus McBride)

The piers of the original Stirling Bridge are beneath the surface of the river in the foreground of this view from the stone footbridge across the Forth. In 1297 a causeway led from the far bank, across the wet meadows, towards the Abbey Craig on which the Wallace Memorial now stands in the right background. (author's photo)

circumstances and a reversion to a fabian strategy. From their rocky eyrie on the Abbey Craig, Wallace and Murray must have watched the comings and goings of the English troops over the bridge with some perplexity. Whether they made any sense of the proceedings or not, the two leaders gave orders for the Scottish army to form for battle. The army had camped in the woodland between the Abbey Craig and the Ochil Hills for the past few nights. It was a place of concealment and might have offered cover and an escape route to the hills in case of defeat, but it was no place to deploy masses of troops into battle array. The Scots emerged from the woods and formed into their fighting formations below the Abbey Craig, in full view of the English. Barely a mile away, the English commanders watched the deployment of the Scots from the battlements of Stirling Castle. Both Warenne and Cressingham underestimated the strength and fighting capabilities of the Scots, although in their defence it could be said that recent Scots performances had done little to disabuse them of this notion. Warenne was not to know that the Scots that Wallace and Murray had brought to Stirling were a far cry from the disorganised rabble that he had so easily put to flight at Dunbar. Several of the more experienced knights present, Richard Lundie among them, were uneasy at what they saw across the river and realised the need for caution.

A Council of War

Warenne called his bannerets to a council of war, the Scottish knight Richard Lundie, who had joined the English after Irvine seems to have been one of the few men of sound judgement among those present. He summed up the situation succinctly and warned; 'My lords if we cross the bridge we are dead men. For we can only go over two by two and the enemy are already formed up; their whole army can charge down upon

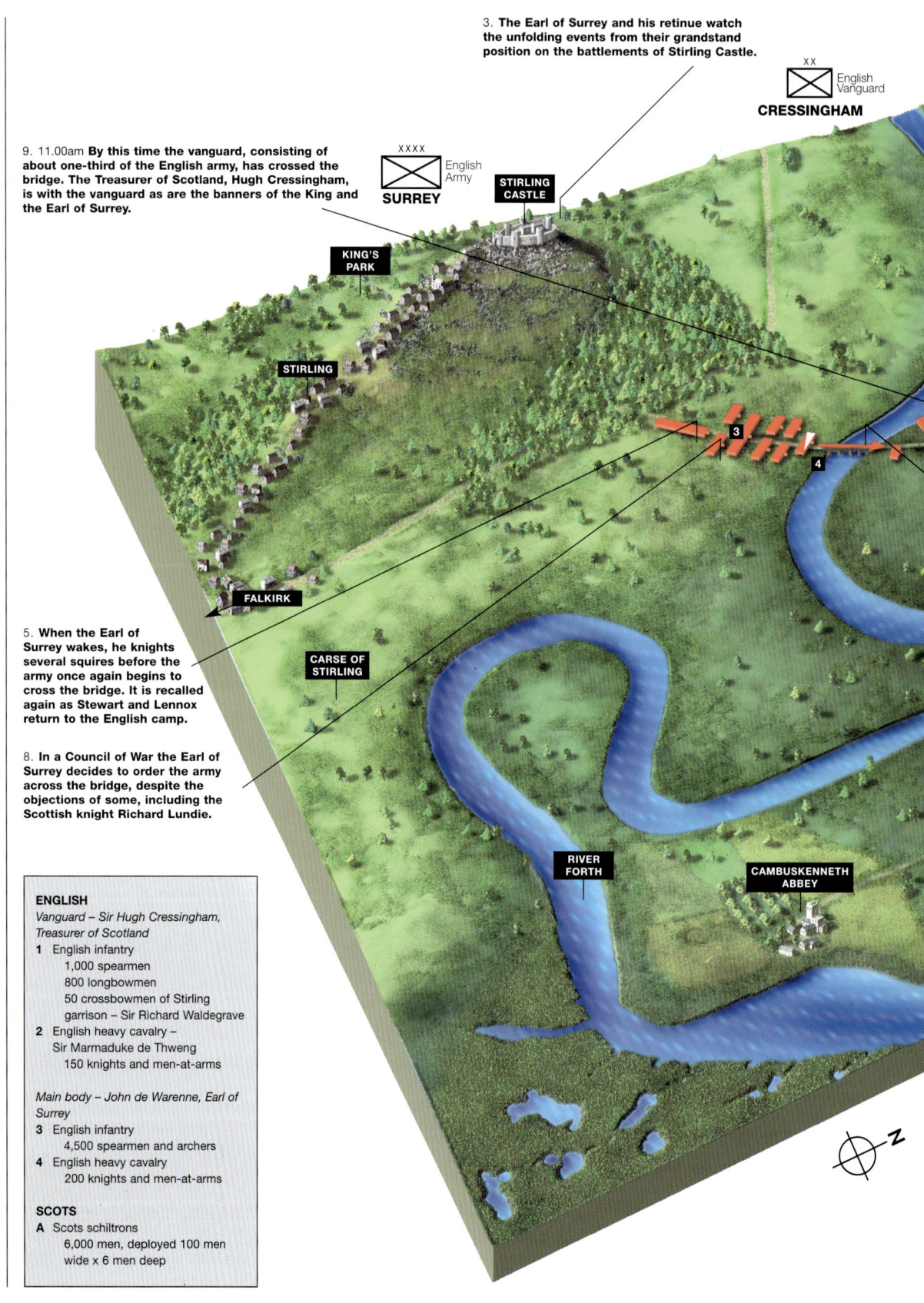

3. **The Earl of Surrey and his retinue watch the unfolding events from their grandstand position on the battlements of Stirling Castle.**

X X
English Vanguard
CRESSINGHAM

9. 11.00am **By this time the vanguard, consisting of about one-third of the English army, has crossed the bridge. The Treasurer of Scotland, Hugh Cressingham, is with the vanguard as are the banners of the King and the Earl of Surrey.**

X X X X
English Army
SURREY

STIRLING CASTLE

KING'S PARK

STIRLING

3

4

FALKIRK

5. **When the Earl of Surrey wakes, he knights several squires before the army once again begins to cross the bridge. It is recalled again as Stewart and Lennox return to the English camp.**

CARSE OF STIRLING

8. **In a Council of War the Earl of Surrey decides to order the army across the bridge, despite the objections of some, including the Scottish knight Richard Lundie.**

RIVER FORTH

CAMBUSKENNETH ABBEY

ENGLISH
Vanguard – Sir Hugh Cressingham, Treasurer of Scotland
1 English infantry
1,000 spearmen
800 longbowmen
50 crossbowmen of Stirling garrison – Sir Richard Waldegrave
2 English heavy cavalry – Sir Marmaduke de Thweng
150 knights and men-at-arms

Main body – John de Warenne, Earl of Surrey
3 English infantry
4,500 spearmen and archers
4 English heavy cavalry
200 knights and men-at-arms

SCOTS
A Scots schiltrons
6,000 men, deployed 100 men wide x 6 men deep

N

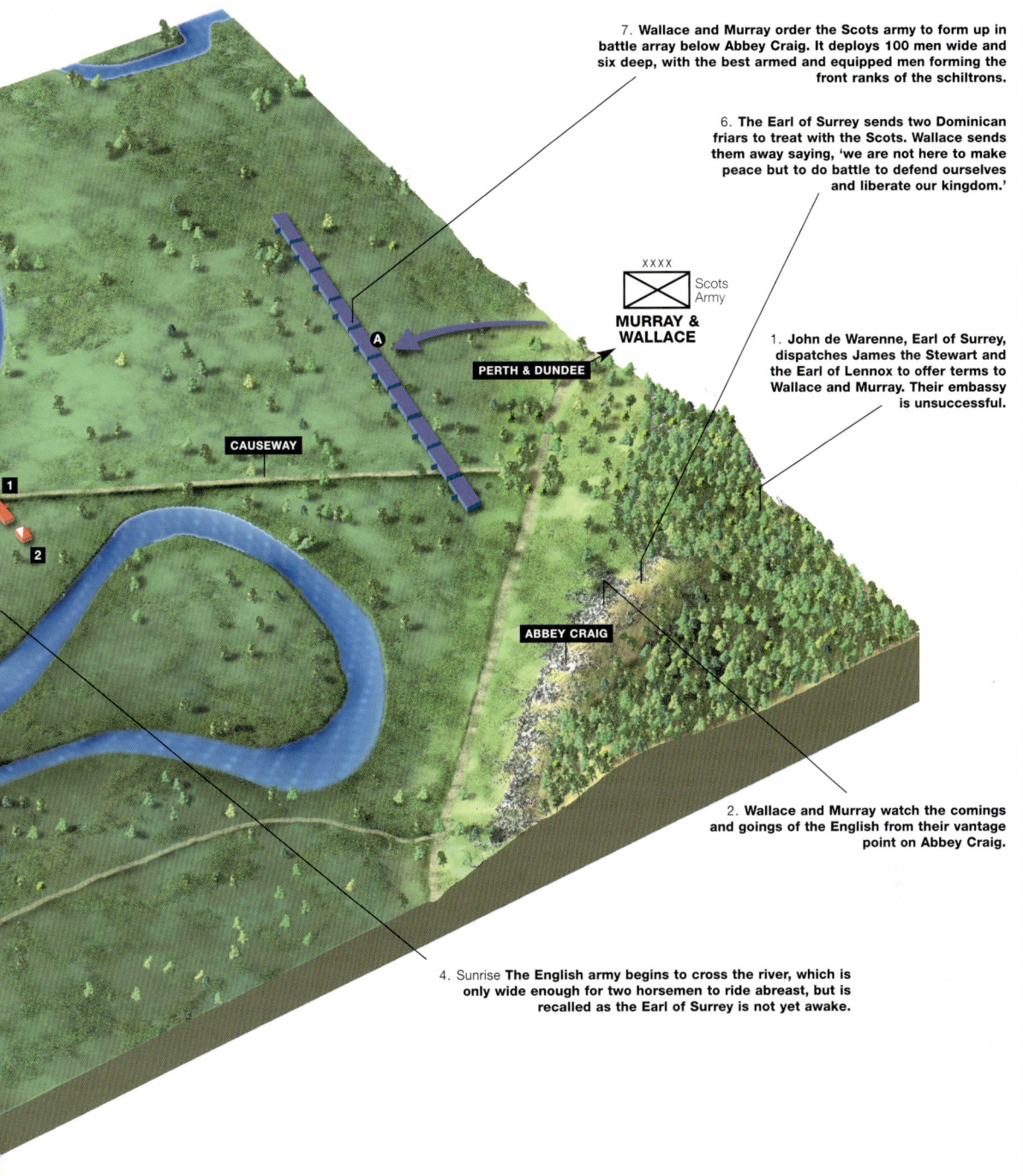

7. Wallace and Murray order the Scots army to form up in battle array below Abbey Craig. It deploys 100 men wide and six deep, with the best armed and equipped men forming the front ranks of the schiltrons.

6. The Earl of Surrey sends two Dominican friars to treat with the Scots. Wallace sends them away saying, 'we are not here to make peace but to do battle to defend ourselves and liberate our kingdom.'

XXXX

Scots Army

MURRAY & WALLACE

PERTH & DUNDEE

1. John de Warenne, Earl of Surrey, dispatches James the Stewart and the Earl of Lennox to offer terms to Wallace and Murray. Their embassy is unsuccessful.

CAUSEWAY

1

2

ABBEY CRAIG

2. Wallace and Murray watch the comings and goings of the English from their vantage point on Abbey Craig.

4. Sunrise The English army begins to cross the river, which is only wide enough for two horsemen to ride abreast, but is recalled as the Earl of Surrey is not yet awake.

STIRLING BRIDGE – THE ENGLISH VANGUARD ADVANCES

11 September 1297, mid-morning, viewed from the southeast, showing the opening moves of the battle as the English Vanguard crosses Stirling Bridge and the Scots move down from the Abbey Craig and deploy to face them.

us whenever they will.' Lundie told them that not far above Stirling, the river was fordable 'sixty at a time' and he asked Warenne to give him a force of horsemen and foot to outflank and fall upon the enemy which would enable the earl to 'cross the bridge in perfect safety'. Cressingham disapproved, the treasurer had already weakened the force available at Stirling by dismissing troops on the grounds of expense and now he chided the earl on the same grounds and arrogantly urged an immediate crossing. 'It will do us no good my lord earl, either to go bickering like this or to waste the king's money in vain manoeuvres. So let us cross over right away and do our duty as we are bound to.' Cressingham wanted the business finished and may have thought that an outflanking movement would simply cause the Scots to melt away into the hills and consequently deny him a part in a victory that would advance his career and enhance his standing with the king. Warenne let himself be swayed by the treasurer, he dispensed with caution and rejected Lundie's advice. The earl may have been wary of dividing his forces, yet there is no evidence that he was short of troops. Had Lundie carried out his outflanking movement in sufficient force then this would have thrown the Scots off balance and forced them to counter his threat. It was a course of action that would have thrown the outcome of the battle into doubt and could have given the English victory. Warenne's decision was ill-judged and Guisborough's comments reflect what must have been Lundie's thoughts; 'Thus, amazing though it is to relate and terrible as was to be its outcome, all these experienced men, though they knew the enemy was at hand, began to cross a bridge so narrow that even two horsemen could scarcely and with much difficulty ride side by side and so they did all morning, without let or hindrance, until the vanguard was on one side of the river and the remainder of the army on the other. There was, indeed, no better place in all the land to deliver the English into the hands of the Scots, and so many into the power of the few.'

About a third of the English army, both foot and horse, had crossed the narrow bridge by 11.00am, with Cressingham and the banners of

The River Forth between the tidal limit and the junction with the River Teith flows wide and deep. In this area, Richard Lundie told John de Warenne, 'the river was fordable sixty at a time.' Stirling Castle is visible beyond the river in the centre. (author's photo)

The old bridge across the Forth at Drip replaced the ford here and has in its turn been rendered obsolete by road development. (author's photo)

the king and the earl to the fore. The vanguard consisted of about 2,000 men, including probably just over 100 horsemen and a strong force of Welsh foot. The redoubtable Yorkshire knight Marmaduke de Thweng crossed with the cavalry as did the constable of Stirling Castle, Richard Waldegrave and many of his garrison troops.

Deliberations of the Scots

The Scottish leaders must have realised that, as the English troops began to form up on the north side of the river for the third time that morning, this crossing was in earnest. The time scale that morning hardly allows for the previous crossings to have been on a large scale and it is probable that the enemy troops were withdrawn before enough had passed over the bridge to invite an attack. The comings and goings would have had the effect of alerting the Scots leaders to what might be the English course of action and gave them time to discuss a riposte. A council of war was probably called to allow the most experienced Scottish officers to discuss the situation, much as Warenne had done on the other side of the river. In this case, however, sound sense and

Old Stirling Bridge is a narrow medieval stone bridge across the River Forth, now used as a footbridge. It stands a matter of yards downstream from the site of the original bridge. Stirling Castle dominates the skyline above the town in the background. In the Middle Ages Scotland was imagined to be divided by water, crossable only at the bridge of Stirling. (author's photo)

45

judgement clearly prevailed. The Scots decided that, rather than stand on the defensive and allow the whole English army to cross the river and attack them, they would take the initiative and attack first, aiming to destroy the enemy vanguard that was so obligingly taking ground in so precarious a situation.

ORDER OF BATTLE

Stirling Bridge, 11 September 1297

THE ENGLISH ARMY
Commander-in-Chief – John de Warenne, Earl of Surrey.

The Fore-Battle or Vanguard
Commanded by Sir Hugh Cressingham, Treasurer of Scotland.

Cavalry
150 knights and troopers on 'covered' or armoured horses, commanded by
Sir Marmaduke de Thweng.

Infantry
1,000 spearmen
800 longbowmen
50 crossbowmen from the castle garrison under Sir Richard Waldegrave.

The Main-Battle and Rear-Battle (neither of which crossed the river or took part in the fighting).
Commanded by Sir William Latimer and Sir Walter Huntercombe.

Cavalry
200 knights and troopers

Infantry
4,500 spearmen and archers

Total: 350 cavalry, 6,350 infantry

THE SCOTTISH ARMY
Commanders of the Army of Scotland – William Wallace, Sir Andrew Murray.

Cavalry
180 knights, troopers and light horsemen

Infantry
6,000 spearmen
400 longbowmen

Total: 180 cavalry, 6,400 infantry

THE SCOTS ATTACK

Packed in tight schiltrons, six ranks deep, 6,000 men were arrayed below the Abbey Craig under the watchful eyes of their commanders on their craggy lookout above. They appeared to the troops of the English vanguard, a little over half a mile away across the flat meadows, as one solid mass of men bristling with bright iron. There were archers from Selkirk

Old Stirling bridge   National Wallace Memorial   Ochil Hills   Abbey Craig

Causwayhead

Forest in support and a small body of about 180 horsemen were held in reserve, perhaps to counter any threat from the flank. Meanwhile, the English cavalry had crossed the river and waited impatiently while the centenars of foot urgently deployed the infantry into line as they debouched from the narrow bridge. Wallace and Murray knew that they must strike soon and drive the enemy into the river before they had concentrated too large a force on the north bank. They did not wish to attack prematurely, wasting the opportunity to destroy or damage a sizable section of the English army. It was a situation that needed a steady commander with fine judgement. We must presume that the moment to attack was a joint decision as the relationship between Wallace and Murray as commanders is obscure. However the decision was taken at the right moment. As the last of the English vanguard of 2,000 men stepped onto the north bank of the Forth the signal to advance was given. The great horns blasted out their call from high on the Abbey Craig and the massed spearmen strode forward with grim determination, the schiltrons bristling with iron-shod pikes like malevolent hedgehogs, their banners flying before them. They came on steadily at first with their officers setting the pace and ordering the ranks. Wallace and Murray rode, fully armed now, with their mounted followers, at their head. About 1,000 yards separated the two armies and most of this distance could be covered at a measured pace without the ranks becoming disordered. The best-armoured among the Scots formed the front ranks of the advancing schiltrons and they

The Abbey Craig and Wallace Monument seen across the River Forth from the esplanade of Stirling Castle with Stirling Bridge in the centre. (author's photo)

47

English vanguard driven into trap formed by loop of river **Old Stirling bridge** **Stirling Castle** **Line of causeway** **Wallace's schiltrons form up on this line**

Stirling Castle seen from Wallace's vantage point on the Abbey Craig. (author's photo)

braced themselves as the first arrows began falling amongst them and men began to fall. At the urgent cry of the signal horns the long spears were levelled for the charge and the schiltrons, gathering momentum, surged eagerly towards the enemy. The bridge was still packed with troops, others were frantically attempting to deploy into some sort of defensive front alongside those who had crossed earlier, some were already wavering as the enveloping Scots bore down on them. Neither the stationary horsemen nor the archers and spearmen could withstand the weight and ferocity of the Scottish onslaught. They were outnumbered, outmanoeuvred and thrust back before the Scottish spears into the trap formed by the loop of river to their rear. The exit from the bridge was soon in Scottish hands and offered no escape route to the packed mass of panicking troops and, with order and discipline breaking down, the Scots cut a bloody swathe through the English making a great slaughter among them. Neither Warenne, Huntercombe, nor Latimer crossed the bridge, nor did the bulk of their troops, they could only look on aghast from the opposite bank as the Scots went about their bloody work. There was no avenue of escape for the trapped vanguard and many of the men-at-arms and an even greater number of the foot perished either at the hands of the Scots or were drowned attempting to cross the river in their cumbersome armour; though at least one knight and his horse, with great difficulty, swam the river fully armoured. The lightly equipped and unarmoured Welsh foot, as many as 300 of them, escaped across the river to safety with less difficulty. Others were not so fortunate, the Constable of Stirling Castle along with many of his garrison troops perished in the disaster; the obese Cressingham, whose seat was at best uncertain, was dragged from his horse and brutally butchered. The Yorkshire knight Marmaduke de Thweng however escaped and salvaged his reputation from the chaos; Guisborough, no doubt, had the tale from the redoubtable warrior himself. Marmaduke watched in dismay as the banners of the king and earl fell beneath the spears of the Scots and realised that the vanguard was lost. He rallied his horsemen and rather than risk drowning by attempting to swim the river he led them through the enveloping ranks of the Scots and across their rear towards the bridge. The impetus of the charge of the heavily armoured men bowled the Scots aside and with Marmaduke at their head they hewed a bloody pathway towards their escape route. At some point Marmaduke's young nephew was brought down as his horse was killed; he cried out for help as the Scots closed in on him. Marmaduke swung down from his mount and hoisted the lad up behind his squire, then remounting he led them hell for leather for the still intact bridge where he and the exhausted remnants of his force fought their way across to safety. Marmaduke's fighting retreat was the last act of organised resistance, the Scots' victory was complete; Warenne and the remains of his army could only look on in dismay as the enemy went about the grim task of finishing off the troops still trapped north of the river.

In a grisly postscript to the battle the Scots took their revenge on the fat treasurer's corpse, and Guisborough tells us that they 'flayed him and divided pieces of his skin between them, not as keepsakes but out of hatred of him'. Then with satisfaction he continues Cressingham's

Stirling Castle from the south-west, across the King's Park. (author's photo)

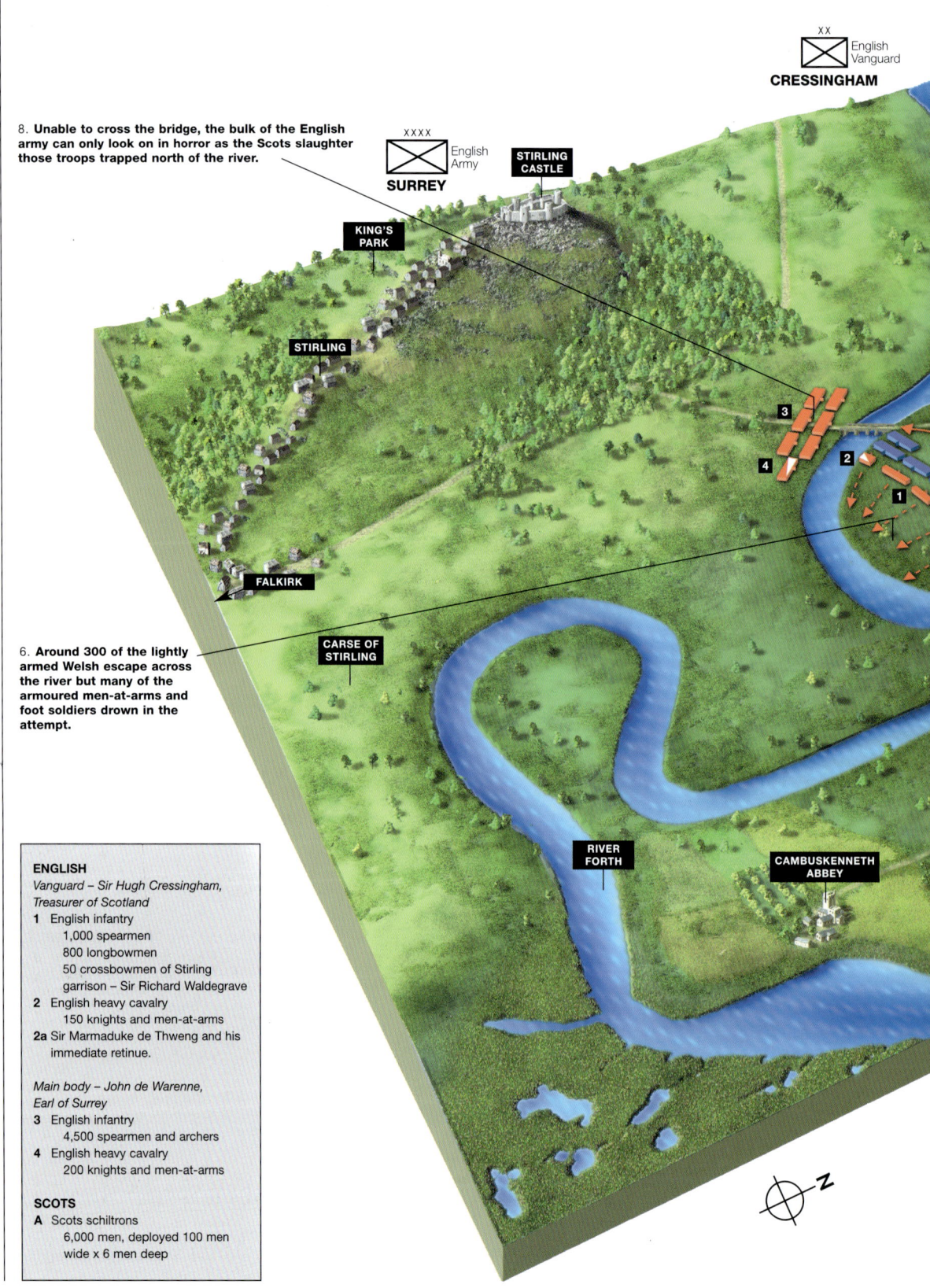

XX English Vanguard
CRESSINGHAM

8. **Unable to cross the bridge, the bulk of the English army can only look on in horror as the Scots slaughter those troops trapped north of the river.**

XXXX English Army
SURREY

STIRLING CASTLE

KING'S PARK

STIRLING

3

4

2

1

FALKIRK

6. **Around 300 of the lightly armed Welsh escape across the river but many of the armoured men-at-arms and foot soldiers drown in the attempt.**

CARSE OF STIRLING

RIVER FORTH

CAMBUSKENNETH ABBEY

N

ENGLISH

Vanguard – Sir Hugh Cressingham, Treasurer of Scotland
1 English infantry
   1,000 spearmen
   800 longbowmen
   50 crossbowmen of Stirling
   garrison – Sir Richard Waldegrave
2 English heavy cavalry
   150 knights and men-at-arms
2a Sir Marmaduke de Thweng and his
   immediate retinue.

Main body – John de Warenne, Earl of Surrey
3 English infantry
   4,500 spearmen and archers
4 English heavy cavalry
   200 knights and men-at-arms

SCOTS
A Scots schiltrons
   6,000 men, deployed 100 men
   wide x 6 men deep

50

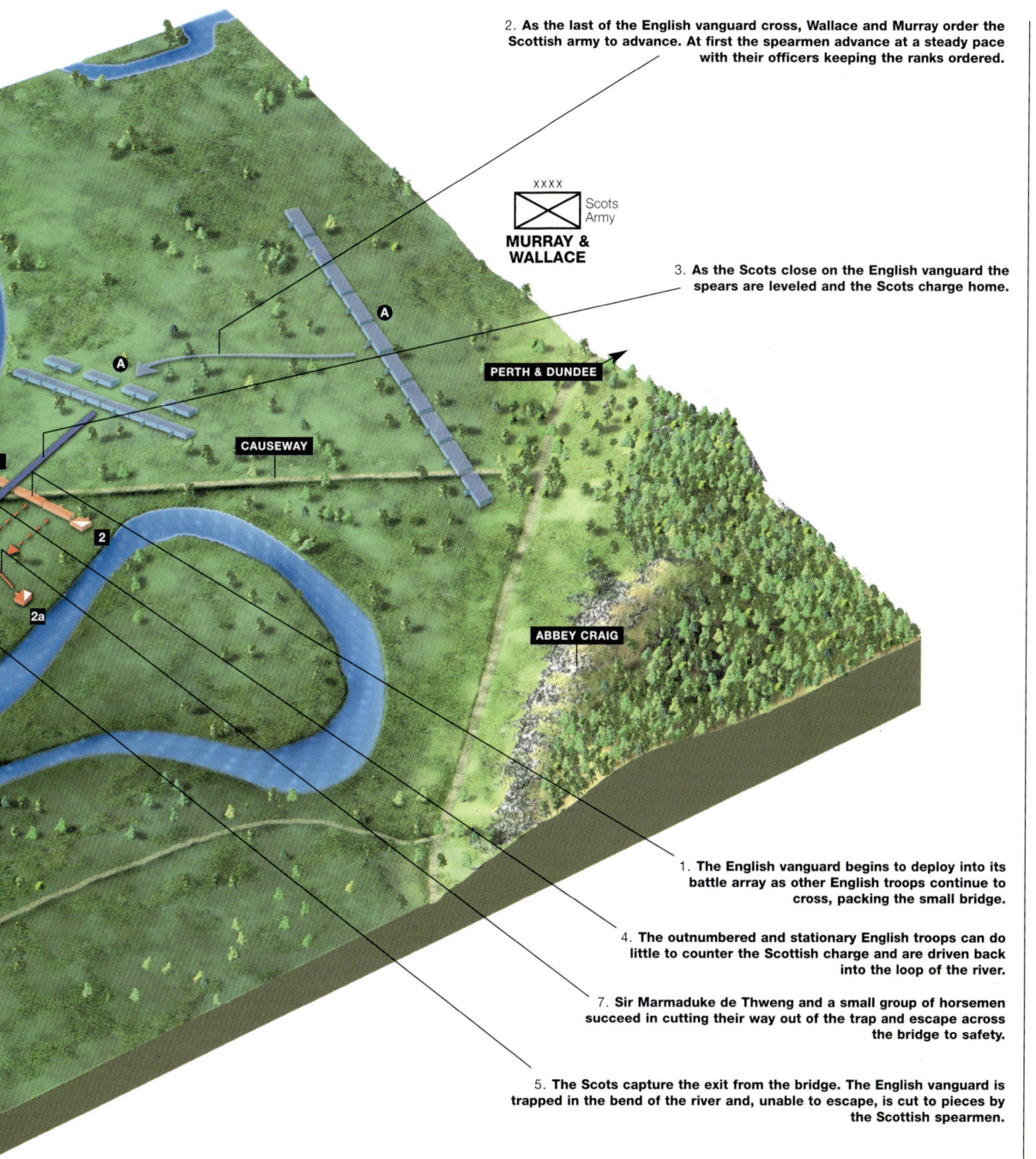

2. **As the last of the English vanguard cross, Wallace and Murray order the Scottish army to advance. At first the spearmen advance at a steady pace with their officers keeping the ranks ordered.**

XXXX
Scots Army

MURRAY & WALLACE

3. **As the Scots close on the English vanguard the spears are leveled and the Scots charge home.**

PERTH & DUNDEE

CAUSEWAY

ABBEY CRAIG

1. **The English vanguard begins to deploy into its battle array as other English troops continue to cross, packing the small bridge.**

4. **The outnumbered and stationary English troops can do little to counter the Scottish charge and are driven back into the loop of the river.**

7. **Sir Marmaduke de Thweng and a small group of horsemen succeed in cutting their way out of the trap and escape across the bridge to safety.**

5. **The Scots capture the exit from the bridge. The English vanguard is trapped in the bend of the river and, unable to escape, is cut to pieces by the Scottish spearmen.**

STIRLING BRIDGE – THE SCOTS ATTACK

11 September 1297, mid-late morning, viewed from the southeast. The trap is sprung as the Scottish spearmen charge the outnumbered and disorganized English Vanguard. With the exit from the bridge captured, the English are trapped north of the river and butchered.

The arms of Hugh Cressingham are not recorded by any contemporary rolls of arms. His seal bore the device of a swan. (author's drawing)

epitaph. 'Of the many who were deceived that day, he was the most deceived, he who was slippery, haughty, proud and addicted to greed'. The flaying of Cressingham seems to have been well-known in England as other accounts, though giving only the barest outline of the battle itself, not only dwell on the subject but embellish the tale with their own gory details.

The fighting had not been entirely one-sided however, for Andrew Murray had been mortally wounded in the battle. His name continued for a time to appear on documents alongside that of Wallace as 'commanders of the army of Scotland', but he seems to have died in early November.

FLIGHT OF THE ENGLISH

Only a part of the English army had been beaten, the larger part had not struck a blow in the fighting, yet it was enough to spell defeat for the whole army as the dispirited English were quite unable to rally and restore the fight despite numbers still superior to the enemy. Warenne had the bridge broken behind him and fled for the safety of Berwick with a strong cavalry escort. He rode with such haste, as Guisborough relates, that his horse 'never again tasted fodder.' He abandoned not only his army but the whole of southern Scotland to its fate and left the north of England open to Scottish reprisal raids. The earl entrusted the defence of Stirling Castle to Marmaduke de Thweng and William Fitzwarin and promised to return with a strong relieving force before the end of the year. Although the garrison was reinforced by Robert de Ros of Wark on Tweed and his retinue the promised relief did not materialise. The castle was not provisioned to withstand a long blockade and soon surrendered to Wallace. Ros was thrown into prison and kept in chains in Dumbarton Castle, Fitzwarin and Thweng were also spared; a chivalrous gesture on the part of Wallace, though no doubt their value as ransomable hostages was a consideration too. Marmaduke was eventually exchanged in April 1299, after more than a year as a prisoner, for the Scots knight John de Moubray who was at that time in English captivity. There is no record of any prisoners from the battle; presumably none were taken. As the English troops abandoned Stirling

The earliest extant drawing of Stirling Castle shows a structure quite different to the buildings we see today. (author's drawing from an early 15th century illustration)

The shattered ruins of Marmaduke de Thweng's castle, high on a wooded bluff above the Kilton Beck in Cleveland, are all that remain today to remind us of this famous warrior. (author's photo)

and marched south, the Stewart, the Earl of Lennox and their followers took the opportunity to desert the defeated English and, now they were certain of Wallace's victory, strike a blow for Scotland themselves. They tailed the dispirited column of English troops as it straggled away towards Falkirk. As the camp followers and the long baggage train bringing up the rear wound across the 'polles', the flat boggy carseland south-east of Stirling, they fell upon them, killing the hapless waggoners, plundering the heavily-laden baggage train and taking great booty. Mounted elements of the Scots army pursued the retreating English, harrying them as they trudged disconsolately towards Berwick, though they were unable to inflict further significant damage on them. Wallace, with the bulk of his men remained in the Stirling area, celebrating and sharing the spoils of victory.

THE AFTERMATH OF STIRLING BRIDGE

The battle of Stirling Bridge and Murray's consequent death in November left Wallace as the undisputed leader of Scotland, a position he retained until after the battle of Falkirk the following July. News of the disaster at Stirling travelled fast and profoundly shocked the English establishment. They responded without delay and as early as the end of September orders were sent out to the sheriff of Nottingham and Derby to send his knights and troopers north to aid Robert Clifford and Brian Fitzalan who were defending the Border as best they could with what local forces were available. Robert Bruce reappeared at this time in arms

Angus McBride '02

STIRLING BRIDGE – THE SCOTS ATTACK THE ENGLISH VANGUARD (pages 54–55)

Led by William Wallace and Andrew Murray, the Scots surge towards Stirling Bridge driving the broken English troops of the Vanguard into the trap formed by a loop of the river. By capturing the bridge the Scots prevented English reinforcements from the opposite bank coming to the aid of the Vanguard. Hugh Cressingham (1), the hated English Treasurer of Scotland, was unsteady in the saddle due to his obesity and fell under the spears of the Scots. In the centre of the painting, he is about to be despatched by Murray (2) and his spearmen. The Earl of Surrey's banner (3), along with that of St George (4) has crossed the river, though the earl himself remained safely on the southern bank with the majority of his troops. The group of mounted knights behind Cressingham includes Marmaduke de Thweng of Kilton Castle in North Yorkshire (5), who eventually fought his way back across the bridge and was the only English knight to emerge from the debacle at Stirling with any credit. Alongside Marmaduke are two other northern knights; Robert Somerville (6) and Richard Waldegrave, the constable of Stirling Castle (7), who was killed along with many of the troops of the garrison. On the Scottish side we know of only Wallace (8) and Murray who fought in the battle. The Stewart and the Earl of Lennox were probably with Warenne during the battle. They took no part in the fighting though they later slipped away to fall on and plunder the retreating English baggage train. The Scot Richard Lundie was firmly in the English camp, his arms, 'three pallets surmounted of a bend charged with as many stars', were deduced from later Lundie seals. Before his precipitate flight from Stirling, Warenne entrusted the castle to the keeping of Marmaduke de Thweng and William Fitzwarin who presumably was present at the battle. We know that Fitzwarin's son John was killed in Scotland, possibly at Stirling Bridge. Fitzwarin was imprisoned after the castle fell to the Scots and was to be exchanged for Henry Seintcler – his wife was travelling to Scotland – but the unfortunate Fitzwarin is recorded as dead in December 1299. William Ros of Wark on Tweed also joined the garrison but we can't be sure that he was up in time for the battle. John de Warenne and his bannerets, Marmaduke de Thweng, William Latimer and Walter Huntercombe, whose banner can be seen on the bridge, had their revenge for the ignominious defeat at Stirling when they fought at Falkirk the following year. Neither Latimer, nor Huntercombe, both well known bannerets, are mentioned in Guisborough's account of Stirling Bridge and they probably never crossed the river. The arms of the unfortunate Hugh Cressingham do not appear in any of the rolls of arms of Edward I, they are derived from a seal of another member of that family. (Angus McBride)

Late in 1297 Wallace attacked the border fortress of Carlisle. Without siege engines, the Scots could make no impression on the defences though they 'burnt the country for thirty leagues around', devastating much of Cumberland. (author's photo)

in the south-west and Clifford raided his lands in Annandale in retaliation for his activities. The Earl of Surrey went straight to London after his evacuation of Scotland, accompanied by Henry Percy, to support the royal cause against Norfolk and Hereford. In October the rift between the king and the earls was patched up, and with the threat of civil war averted, preparations were made to send a large force of horse and foot to Newcastle in response to the situation in the north. Wallace did not immediately follow up his victory at Stirling with an attack on northern England, while the enemy was in disarray, as might have been expected. When he confronted the English outside Berwick late in September he was forced to retire by their reorganised forces arrayed for battle. Nevertheless, Scotland was almost cleared of occupying troops, the castles of Dundee and Stirling resisted for a while, probably surrendering early in 1298, but Edinburgh, Roxburgh and the castle at Berwick held out although the town, which Lanercost reports 'was then without walls', was taken by Henry Haliburton.

Wallace raids the North of England

There were some opportunistic cross-border raids immediately after Stirling Bridge, then in October Wallace himself led an army of about 100 horse and 3,000 foot into Northumberland. The raid was a savage and destructive affair marked by atrocities due to the indiscipline of the Scots troops. They burnt and plundered their way down Tynedale to Corbridge and Hexham, where protection money was extorted from the priory, and then moved west against Cumberland and Carlisle. The Scots could not take the well-fortified Border stronghold without siege engines but cooped up the garrison, including Henry Percy's forces, for a month, with a large blockading force, while they devastated and 'burnt the country for thirty leagues round.' Then, with winter beginning to bite, they marched east towards Durham but, after crossing Stainmore, heavy snow caused them to turn aside at Bowes and make for Newcastle which was less well fortified than Carlisle. But the defence of the town

ABOVE **In November 1297, during the Scottish raid into Northern England, a letter of protection was issued to the monks of the Augustinian priory at Hexham in the names of Andrew de Murray and William Wallace. No doubt the letter was in return for a substantial payment of 'blackmail' or protection money. (author's photo)**

LEFT **Bowes Castle, County Durham. None of the great strongholds of the north fell to Wallace during his destructive invasion into the northern counties of England in 1297. At Bowes the onset of winter brought his incursion into the palatinate to a halt and he turned for home. (author's photo)**

was well organised and the ill-disciplined Scots were wearying of winter campaigning and wanted to return home with their plunder, much of it on the hoof. Wallace had been absent from Scotland long enough and his presence was needed at home. He had no choice; he abandoned his attempt on Newcastle and crossed the Border back into Scotland at the beginning of December. The raid, though destructive, achieved nothing militarily, however it earned the Scots plunder and protection payments that boosted their revenues. It was seen as bringing retribution to the English and above all was a popular move that served to strengthen Wallace's position in Scotland.

At some time during the winter of 1297/98 Wallace was knighted by one of the premier Scottish earls and elected as Guardian of the Realm. His standing among the nobility was thus enhanced and his authority and leadership given official title. We have no details of these events, the only witness to the facts is a charter, one of only four documents known to us from his time of power, in which Wallace styles himself 'knight, Guardian of the kingdom of Scotland and commander of its army, in the name of the famous prince the lord John, by God's grace illustrious king of Scotland, by consent of the community of that realm'. The document was issued to Alexander Scrymgeour in March 1298, sometime after the fall of Dundee castle, giving him custody of the castle and granting him land in return for which he was to pay homage to John Balliol and act as standard bearer to the king. Clearly, Wallace regarded himself as acting on behalf of the exiled Balliol and made no move to set himself up as an independent ruler. The consent of the community that he claims however may not have been wholehearted in the case of the nobility. The only survivor today of these four documents is the letter written to the Hanseatic town of Lubeck on 11 October 1297 in which he invites the resumption of trade, as Scotland 'was now recovered by war from the power of the English'. But the claim was premature, for the disaster at Stirling Bridge had united the English in their determination to bring the Scots to heel and to invade Scotland in 1298.

THE CAMPAIGN OF 1298

Edward summons his forces

There was little King Edward could do to avenge the defeat of his forces at Stirling Bridge before the summer of 1298. Ralph Fitzwilliam was temporarily in command on the Border while awaiting the return of John de Warenne. During the months of December and January his forces amounted to not more than 2,000 local foot, 75 crossbowmen, of whom 15 were mounted, and six northern knights with 40 troopers. Though the king and his army did not return from Flanders until 14 March 1298 preparations for the invasion of Scotland were underway late in 1297 when some 29,000 foot were summoned to assemble at Newcastle early in December but the response was slow and new writs were issued for troops to muster, again at Newcastle, at the end of January. In his Welsh Wars Edward had established the principle of winter campaigning but this was not popular, nevertheless, the bulk of the foot, some 16,000 men, arrived in the first weeks of February some having taken three weeks to march north. By this time Warenne had taken command; he had with him the earls of Norfolk, Hereford and Arundel and many other barons and knights with a cavalry force numbering at least 750 lances. New arrivals brought the total of foot to 21,000 for a short time but it soon dropped to 18,000 and by March to 10,000 and subsequently 5,000. Warenne and his army achieved little other than the relief of the castles of Roxburgh and Berwick, the Scots declined battle and retreated.

Anthony Bek, Bishop of Durham and John Fitzmarmaduke were sent by the king to take certain castles of East Lothian still held by the Scots. One of these was Dirleton Castle, the well-preserved and cared for remains of which are open to visitors. (author's photo)

The king sent orders that he was not to undertake a major campaign until he arrived to take command in person. Large as Warenne's army was, it was of poor quality and most of the men were soon dismissed. During April and May there remained only about 1,500 foot and 100 horse to defend the Border. King Edward planned to advance into Scotland with better troops in the summer and to this end he issued new writs of summons. Only 2,000 English foot were called, 1,000 men from each of the counties of Cheshire and Lancashire. The extant writs suggest that Guisborough was right that practically all the infantry of the army at Falkirk were Welsh, as Edward summoned a total of 10,500 Welsh troops, the best fighting men he had. There were 250 crossbowmen still in pay from Warenne's humbled army along with a further 250–300 Gascon mercenaries whom we can assume were crossbowmen too, some of whom were mounted. The records show that the horse were in greater numbers than in Flanders. Many of the retinues were reorganised for the Falkirk campaign and new knights with their followers enrolled besides. Many who were *valetti* (esquires) in Flanders were knighted for the Scottish campaign. Gascon mercenaries such as the Captal de Buch enrolled their retinues for the campaign as did the Frenchman Henry de Beaumont, who played so prominent a role in the later wars against Scotland. There were about 2,200 cavalry altogether, of whom 1,200 were in pay and 1,000 were feudal retinues. The army that Edward raised for the Falkirk campaign bears no comparison to that of Stirling Bridge. The contemporary roll of Falkirk is a roll call of the chivalry of England, it lists 11 earls, the Prince Bishop of Durham, Henry of Lancaster, Aymer de Valence, Robert Clifford, Henry Percy and many other famous names among the 115 bannerets who were with the king; clearly Wallace was seen as a threat not to be taken lightly.

King Edward meant business in 1298, nothing less than the complete subjugation of Scotland. He moved the headquarters of government to York where it was to remain for the next six years. He arrived in York with his household troops on 26 May from where he made a pilgrimage to the shrine of John of Beverley, a saint popular with the army who held his name to be especially potent in battle. He took the saint's banner with him and proceeded by way of Wilton, Kirkham and Northallerton to Durham, where he arrived on 12 June. Here, to the banner of John of Beverley, he added the banner of Cuthbert of Durham, a saint whose reputation as a defender of the English against the Scots vied with that of the divine John. These were the same ancient banners that had inspired the English at Northallerton in 1138, now Edward in turn had enlisted

The imposing ruins of Tantallon Castle, overlooking the Firth of Forth and the Bass Rock, stand on the site of an earlier structure, one of the castles of East Lothian that Bishop Bek set out to capture in 1298. (author's photo)

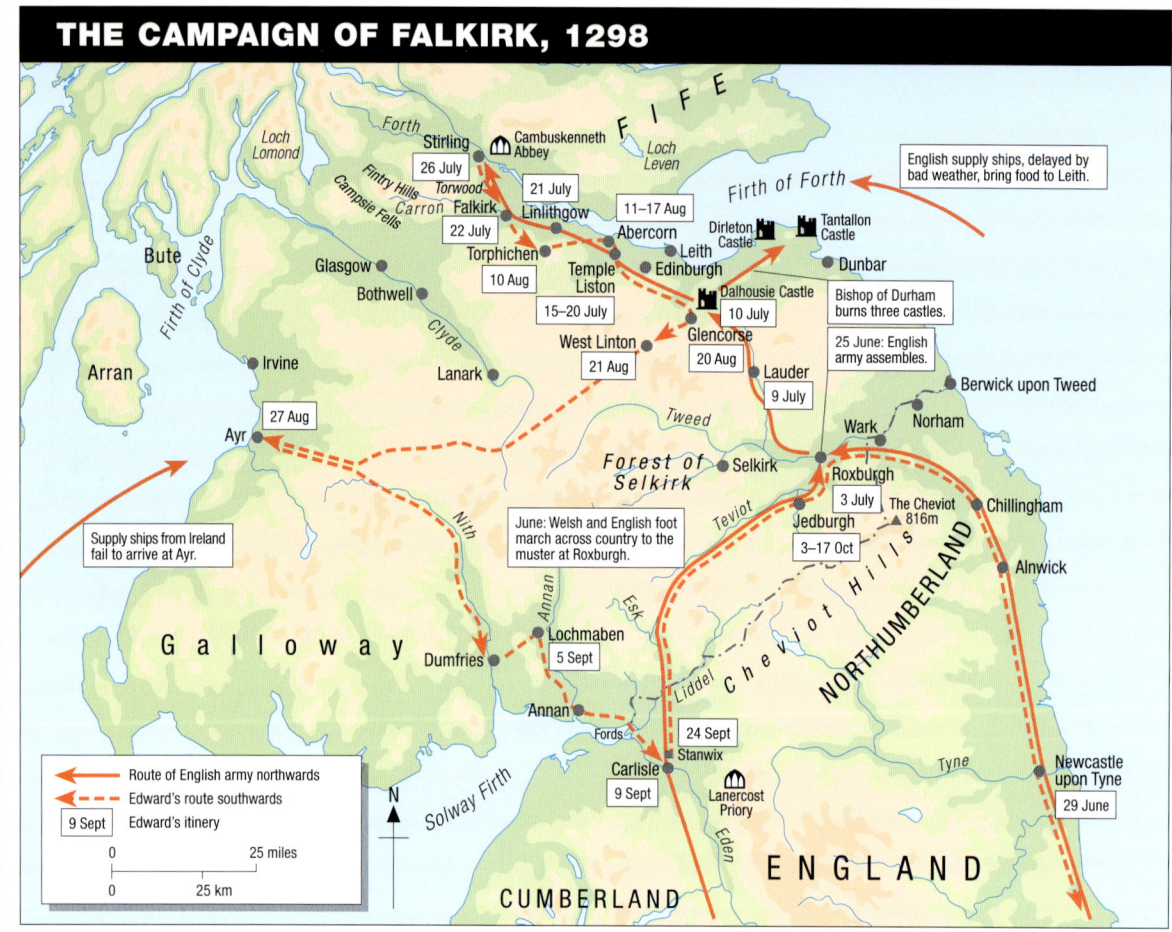

English supply ships, delayed by bad weather, bring food to Leith.

Bishop of Durham burns three castles.

25 June: English army assembles.

June: Welsh and English foot march across country to the muster at Roxburgh.

Supply ships from Ireland fail to arrive at Ayr.

Route of English army northwards
Edward's route southwards
Edward's itinerary

0   25 miles
0   25 km

the saints on his side and their sacred banners would be carried before the army on the forthcoming campaign. English propaganda at this time was loud in its denunciation of Wallace's alleged crimes and sought to vilify him in popular imagination.

Meanwhile, as far as we know, in the spring and early summer of 1298 Wallace was in the wild country of Selkirk Forest, gathering and training an army to oppose the invasion he knew would come that year. He realised that to oppose a full-scale invasion led by King Edward himself he would need not only trained men but large numbers of them. There is evidence that he did not scruple to use force to dragoon the unwilling into service and it is said that he had gallows erected outside towns as a warning to shirkers. Large armies have big appetites and it cannot have been easy for Wallace to keep so many men together over an extended period of time. It is probable that as his numbers increased he moved his base to the Torwood where he could more easily supply his troops and sit astride Edward's route to Stirling.

The king rode from Durham to Newcastle where he stayed until 29 June. Then he moved north to Alnwick and thence by way of Chillingham to Roxburgh, where he joined the army early in July. The cavalry assembled at Roxburgh at midsummer, 25 June, where it joined the infantry that had come across country from Carlisle. Then the whole army, with the king at its head, marched north through the Lammermuir

Hills by way of Lauderdale. The area through which the English advanced was quite devoid of inhabitants and sustenance as the Scots had fled and destroyed everything of use in their path. The English added to the destruction and the black columns of smoke that marked their progress taunted Wallace to dare to oppose their advance. Edward had no intelligence of the whereabouts of the main Scottish army but pressed on through Lauderdale then by way of Dalhousie to Kirkliston, to the west of Edinburgh, where he remained from 15 to 20 July. The army was accompanied by a long train of supply waggons as well as livestock on the hoof, which brought up the rear. Edward was a past master of logistics, his conquest of Wales had been due to good organisation rather than decisive military actions. Yet in 1298 the failure of his supply arrangements brought the campaign near to disaster. The march from Roxburgh must have exhausted the food accompanying the army and the advance stalled at Kirkliston in some discomfort. Bad weather and contrary winds had delayed the ships that were bringing much needed food to Leith from the east coast ports of England. It was no easy matter to feed an army – the quantities required were vast. The prior of Coldstream claimed £177.17s for the night that the English army spent at his priory when they first invaded Scotland. That night, taking advantage of the prior's well-stocked larder, the prodigious appetite of the army accounted for £50 of corn, 497 ewes with lambs and 100 sheep! While the army waited hungrily at Kirkliston, Edward sent Antony Bek, Bishop of Durham, and John Fitzmarmaduke to take certain castles of East Lothian still held by the Scots. The bishop's men had nothing but peas and beans from the fields for rations and without siege engines Bek was doubtful of success. He sent Fitzmarmaduke back to the king with a message to that effect and asked for new instructions. Edward reproached the bishop in his reply, telling him that, 'Christian piety has no place in what he is doing now.' He urged Bek to be ruthless and made it clear that he would countenance no half measures and that he was determined to make an end of the Scots by whatever means were necessary, 'be off, use all your cruelty, and instead of rebuking you I shall praise you. Take care you don't see me until all three castles are burnt.' The timely arrival of some of the overdue supply ships both fed and encouraged the troops and spurred on by the king's angry words Bek's men took Dirleton Castle within two days, after which the Scots evacuated the remaining castles without a fight. But some of the supply ships had brought wine, 200 tuns of it, not the urgently awaited food that contrary winds still delayed. Many of the Welsh infantry were now in a desperate plight from hunger. Somehow or other the Welsh got at the drink and, predictably, trouble ensued and fighting broke out between them and the English infantry. A number of priests, perhaps attempting to quell the riot, became involved in the brawl and were set upon and killed by the drink-crazed Welshmen. This led to the intervention of the English men-at-arms who laid into the drunks with gusto leaving 80 of them dead before order was restored. The Welsh, bloodied and sullen, withdrew some distance from the English to angrily lick their wounds. Edward's campaign had at this point reached its nadir. It is unlikely that the whole Welsh contingent was involved in the disturbance however; there was little unity among the Welsh and many divisions between them. Edward himself was unimpressed when told next morning of their threat to desert to the

The effigy of Gilbert d'Umfraville, Earl of Angus (1245–1307) shows the ravages of time and now lies neglected in Hexham Priory Church. The Umfravilles were in fact English, lords of Prudhoe Castle and of Coquetdale and Redesdale. At Falkirk, Gilbert served with the Bishop of Durham and brought with him a retinue of seven knights and 14 troopers. (drawn by Pete Armstrong)

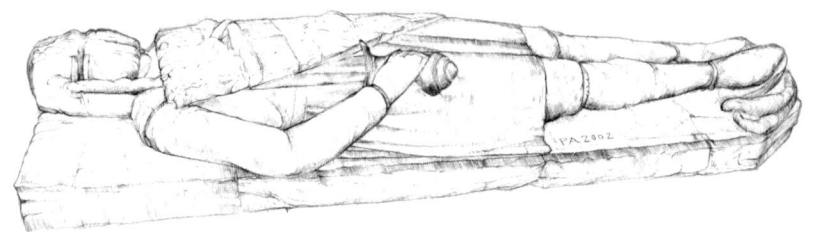

The effigy of John Fitzmarmaduke at Chester-le-Street, Co. Durham; the shield bears his arms, 'argent, a fess between three popinjays gules.' (drawn by Pete Armstrong)

Scots. Let them join the Scots he retorted, 'we shall then defeat the whole lot of them in one go'. Despite his blustering confidence Edward's campaign was going badly and he decided to retire on Edinburgh to resupply the army. Edward it seems had no idea where the Scots army was, and judging by the warnings sent to the sheriffs of Northumberland, Cumberland and Westmorland he feared that Wallace might launch a counter-invasion by way of the West March. In fact Wallace's army was at this time somewhere to the west of the English, standing between them and their objective, Stirling Castle.

At this low point in English fortunes two Scottish earls, Patrick of Dunbar and Gilbert d'Umfraville, Earl of Angus, both Scottish by title but English in all other respects, came to Edward with a scout or spy, who told the king that the Scots were just outside Falkirk, no more than 18 miles away, 'They have heard that you intend to retreat to Edinburgh, and they mean to follow you and attack your camp tomorrow night, or at least to fall on your rearguard and plunder your vanguard.' From this it appears that Wallace's intention was not to wait and fight a pitched battle but to harry the retreating English, perhaps hoping to turn retreat into headlong flight. On hearing this news the king was galvanised into action and, declaring that he would 'not trouble them to seek me', he gave orders for an immediate advance in the direction of Falkirk, though without making his intentions known to his men it seems. The English may have been low on supplies but they were far from a beaten and retreating army. They had yet to strike a blow and some food must have been hastened up from Leith, enough for a day or so, as we hear no more of hunger, only of marching and battle; Wallace had misjudged his enemy. It was early afternoon by the time the army left Kirkliston, they covered the ten miles or so to their camping ground on the Burgh Muir, east of Linlithgow, at a steady unhurried pace. It was late when they arrived and Guisborough tells us that they spent the night in arms, 'arranging their shields as pillows and their arms as coverlets. Their horses too, tasted nothing save hard steel, and were tethered each one hard by his lord.' In the middle of the night the king's charger, carelessly watched by a squire, trod on the sleeping king, injuring him. A commotion ensued and a cry arose in the camp that the enemy was upon them and the men arose and took up their arms ready for action. The king was only slightly hurt however and the situation was soon restored, but the camp was awake and the fighting spirit of the troops had been aroused. So, painfully, Edward mounted his charger and set out with the army towards Falkirk long before the break of dawn.

THE BATTLE OF FALKIRK

The Terrain and Site

The site of the battle of Falkirk is not marked on Ordnance Survey maps of the area as there is no agreement on its location. The landscape around Falkirk is not characterised by strong geographical features, much less by the landmarks that so clearly define the site of the battle of Stirling Bridge. Nor are the contemporary chronicles very illuminating. Guisborough, who provides us with the most information says only that the Scots were formed 'on hard ground and on one side of a hillock, next to Falkirk.' The *Scalacronica* of Sir Thomas Gray says even less, 'they fought on this side of Falkirk' and the Westminster chronicler writes of 'the plain which is called Falkirk'. The known facts can be made to fit a number of sites, traditionally the site was considered to be north of the town but more recent opinion has inclined towards the south. One possible site is at Glen Ellrig, on the River Avon, although it is rather far south of the town for a battle fought there to be called the battle of Falkirk, the site fits the facts, if, as Blind Harry would have us believe, the English army camped on Slamannan Muir on the night before the battle.

The most probable route of the English army from Kirkliston, and one that agrees closely with Guisborough's account, is by way of Winchburgh towards Linlithgow, where they camped nearby on the Burgh Muir. Before dawn the army crossed the River Avon near Manuel Priory, passed by Hayning Castle, then took to the high ground by way of Maddiston and the track along the ridge towards Redding Muir which may have been where 'they saw many spearmen on the brow of the hill.' At first light, from this vantage point, they made out the Scottish army in the distance, just over a mile away to the north-west. Their position

The advance of the Earl of Lincoln's vanguard was delayed by a boggy loch in the bottom of the valley beyond the railway. The site of this is apparently no more visible today from the slopes above the Glen Burn than it was in 1298. (author's photo)

Valley of Glen Burn — Callendar Wood — Boggy Loch — Scots position on ridge — Westquarter Burn runs in trees — Railway

ABOVE **The upper reaches of the Westquarter Burn where the English vanguard crossed followed by the fourth brigade of cavalry under the Earl of Surrey. (author's photo)**

ABOVE, RIGHT **The Westquarter Burn east of the junction with the Glen Burn. It was in this area that the Bishop of Durham's brigade crossed the Burn and the altercation with Ralph Basset took place. (author's photo)**

was on the south-east facing slope of a hillside above the Westquarter Burn with an impassable bog below in the valley bottom that had formed at the confluence of the Westquarter and Glen Burns. Behind the Scots position were the woods of Callendar and further beyond was the town of Falkirk. The bog was certainly an obstacle but could be avoided easily enough simply by skirting round it. It was not part of the Scottish defensive position. The open slopes above, where the schiltrons stood, were firm ground and offered no impediment to the heavy cavalry. The lay of the land, in particular the rather steep bank rising from the boggy area, invited a flank attack. Callendar Wood, to the rear of the Scots, would have offered an escape route in case of defeat, otherwise there seems to be no obvious defensive advantages to the position. By opting to fight a defensive battle Wallace had surrendered the initiative to Edward without the compensating advantage of a strong position. We don't know for what reason Wallace decided to fight at Falkirk but there is a strong possibility that he only became aware of Edward's advance from Kirkliston when his scouts (or perhaps the spearmen whom the English had mistaken for the Scottish army) brought the alarming news that the enemy were nearby on the ridge of Redding Muir. Wallace would have realised then that somehow the fog of war had allowed Edward to steal a march on him. By then it would have been too late to retreat, a move which in the face of the advancing cavalry would have invited disaster, there was only time to form the schiltrons, not on ground that Wallace would have chosen to fight on, but in the best position available in the circumstances.

Contemporary sources for the battle of Falkirk

Walter of Guisborough's graphic account of the battle of Falkirk is the most detailed and accurate contemporary one we have; it has an internal consistency and the facts that we can check against other sources, such as the names of the commanders of the English cavalry brigades and the presence of Ralf Basset in the Bishop of Durham's brigade, are confirmed by the Falkirk roll and other documents.

Guisborough's information came from someone well-placed and close to events, almost certainly an eyewitness, perhaps a banneret or knight of the household or a cleric in royal service. Several prominent Yorkshire knights fought at Falkirk and may have told Walter their tale. The Lanercost chronicle account is short and so is that of the *Scalacronica*; they contribute only the odd additional detail. Other chroniclers follow Guisborough's account word for word. Walter Bower, writing later, astonishingly, blames Robert Bruce for the defeat and Blind Harry's versifying weaves a tortuous tale that leaves Wallace the victor. My account incorporates the landscape features of the Westquarter Burn site with the account of Walter of Guisborough, which it follows closely.

THE SCOTS SIGHTED – DAWN, 22 JULY 1298

In the grey light of dawn on 22 July the vanguard of the English army, after a pre-dawn march from their encampment on the Borough Muir near Linlithgow, at last caught sight of the Scots. On the crest of Redding Muir, ahead of them and on their line of march, appeared a large body of spearmen. Believing that the whole Scottish army was in position on the ridge beyond, the English hastily formed into battle order and advanced up the slope ahead, but, on cresting the ridge they found no sign of the enemy. They halted and a tent was set up to serve as a chapel; it was the day of the Magdalene, and the King and the Bishop of Durham celebrated a mass in the saint's honour. By the time the sacred rites were over the day was beginning to brighten and the men could see more clearly. In the distance, just over a mile to the north-west, the Scots could be seen drawing up in battle formation and preparing to fight.

Disposition of the armies
The Scots spearmen were massed into four great circles, 'which circles are called schiltrouns', Guisborough tells us. He says nothing of any defensive stakes that may have been planted in front of the spearmen, only that 'in these circles the spearmen were settled, with their

View from the bridge over the Union Canal towards the crest of Redding Muir. The cavalry brigades of the earls of Lincoln and Surrey advanced from the ridge, at centre-left, crossed the Westquarter Burn, marked by the trees in the middle-distance and descended the slope in the foreground towards the valley bottom. (author's photo)

Westquarter Burn in dip **Boggy Loch** **Callendar Wood** **Woodend Farm/Scots postition**

lances raised obliquely; linked each one with his neighbour, and their faces turned towards the circumference of the circle'. I don't think Guisborough's reference that the spearmen were 'linked each one with his neighbour' implies a physical link. Rather he means to suggest a very solid defensive formation such as that employed by the spearmen of North Wales. It was by means of this 'human fortress' that Wallace intended to withstand the English onslaught. Clearly the spearmen were formed up in circles with the expectation of an attack from all sides, implying that the flanks of the Scottish army were not anchored on any physical features but were rather 'in the air'. In the spaces between the four schiltrons, each made up of about 2,000 spearmen, were arrayed bodies of archers from the forest of Selkirk. They were longbowmen, equal in every way, excepting their numbers, to their opponents; 'Men of fine build and tall stature' Guisborough admiringly calls them. 'And at the back, on the extreme flank, were their knights'; I take this to mean that the cavalry were together in one body, in reserve behind one flank of the schiltrons. It is difficult to envisage the role that Wallace had in mind for his cavalry, they were drawn up in a vulnerable, open position, their presence, as the opening moves of the battle were to prove, invited the attack of the far stronger English cavalry.

The Comyns and other earls who supported Wallace had contributed much of this mounted force and, though they themselves were absent, many of the lesser Scottish gentry were present. These men, despite their poor showing at Falkirk, would oppose the English and provide the core of support for Robert Bruce in the years to come. It has been suggested that Bruce was among these knights but the evidence of his whereabouts at this time is inconclusive. Nor can we be definite about who led the Scottish cavalry but the probability is that it was James, the High Steward.

The Scottish array stood on a dry, sloping hillside facing slightly east of south with the wood of Callendar to their rear and the town of Falkirk some distance away to the north-west, not, it must be admitted as Guisborough tells us, on the Scottish flank. The hillside sloped away towards the shallow valley where the Glen Burn joins the Westquarter Burn; here in the waterlogged valley bottom, in front of the Scottish line, a sodden morass had formed that, after heavy rain, became a boggy lake.

ORDER OF BATTLE

Falkirk, 22 July 1298

THE ENGLISH ARMY
Commander-in-Chief – King Edward I

Cavalry

The Vanguard
Commanded by the Earl of Lincoln (3 earls, 18 bannerets)
450 bannerets, knights and troopers

The Second Brigade
Commanded by Anthony Bek, Bishop of Durham (1 prince bishop, 2 earls, 24 bannerets)
425 bannerets, knights and troopers

The Third Brigade
Commanded by King Edward I (2 earls, 43 bannerets)
850 bannerets, knights and troopers
100 mounted Crossbowmen

The Fourth Brigade
Commanded by John de Warenne, Earl of Surrey (4 earls, 15 bannerets)
425 bannerets, knights and troopers

Infantry
5,500 longbowmen
7,000 spearmen
400 crossbowmen

Total: 2,250 cavalry, 12,900 Infantry.

Note: The total of cavalry is probably accurate but there is no record of how many of the infantry summoned for the campaign actually took part. Disaffection among the Welsh may have resulted in a high level of desertion in addition to normal wastage.

THE SCOTTISH ARMY
Commander-in-Chief – Sir William Wallace, Guardian of Scotland.

Cavalry
Commanded by James the High Steward.
500 knights and troopers

Infantry
8,000 spearmen organised into 4 schiltrons
1,500 longbowmen, commanded by Sir John Stewart

Total: 500 cavalry, 9,500 infantry.

THE ENGLISH HEAVY CAVALRY ATTACK

When King Edward saw the situation he hesitated and suggested that, rather than attack immediately, they should pitch their tents and feed the men and their horses as they had eaten nothing since setting off from Kirkliston the previous afternoon. But his commanders and close advisors would have nothing of this delay, saying that it was not safe, 'for between these two armies there is nothing but a very small stream.'

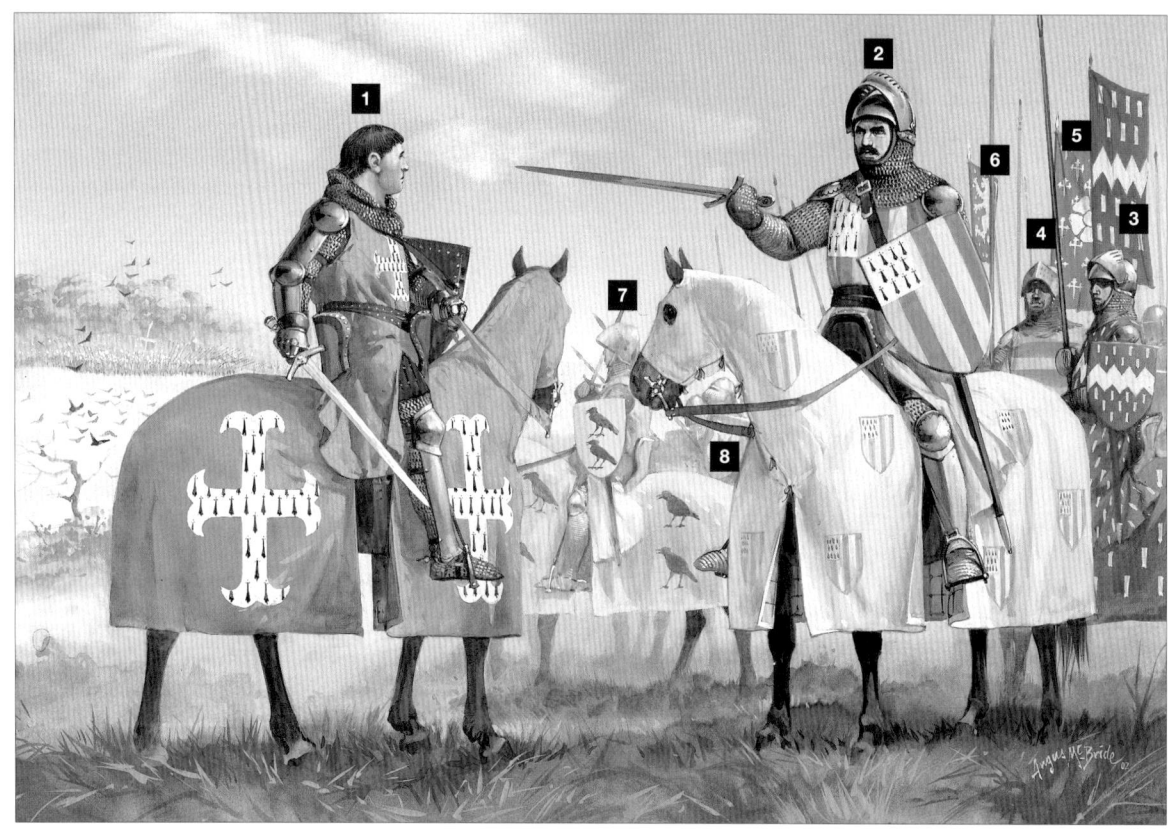

ANTHONY BEK, BISHOP OF DURHAM, AT THE BATTLE OF FALKIRK (pages 70–71)

Anthony Bek, Bishop of Durham (1), commanding the second cavalry brigade, orders his knights to check their advance at the Westquarter Burn and await the king with his horsemen before pressing home their attack on the Scots. Ralph Basset of Drayton (2) arrogantly chides the bishop for what he sees as timidity: 'Go and celebrate mass if you will, for on this day we will do the fighting.' After the exchange Bek's impetuous knights rode on heedless of the bishop towards the dense schiltrons of spearmen on the hillside beyond. Behind Sir Ralph, Edmund Deincourt (3) and Brian FitzAlan of Bedale (4), await the outcome of the confrontation, in their group are the banners of Gilbert de Umfraville, the Northumbrian Earl of Angus (5), an experienced campaigner who fought in the Barons' War in the 1260s and William Braose, Lord of Gower (6). Beyond the bishop are Piers Corbet (7) and John Peynell, Lord of Otley in Yorkshire (8), who had recently returned with the king from Flanders; both these knights had seen hard service in the Welsh wars. Anthony Bek was a younger son of John Bek of Eresby in Lincolnshire and being well connected, he rose rapidly in the ranks of the clergy and was consecrated Bishop of Durham in 1284. In his time the power of the bishops of Durham as lords palatine reached its zenith. From early manhood he was a counsellor and friend of Edward I and is sometimes called his secretary as he was engaged continuously in his service, accompanying him on crusade and serving as an ambassador in France, Flanders, Wales and Scotland. The Durham historian Graystanes tells how he was seen by his contemporaries: 'This Anthony was of lofty disposition; second to none in the kingdom in splendour, dress and military power; concerned rather with the business of the kingdom rather than the affairs of his bishopric; a strong support to the king in war and provident in counsel.' He was constable of the Tower of London and later the Pope made him Patriarch of Jerusalem and Edward made him King of Man. His later years were embittered by feuds with both the king and the Pope. He died in 1311 and was buried in Durham Cathedral, the first bishop to be buried within its walls since St Cuthbert. At Falkirk the bishop's personal following or retinue consisted of 19 knights, five troopers and three clerks. The insubordinate Ralph Basset of Drayton in Staffordshire was a prominent soldier who had served in the Welsh Wars with the Earl of Surrey. He rode a dun warhorse worth 50 marks at Falkirk and brought two knights and nine troopers to the battle, none of whom lost a horse during the fighting, suggesting that neither Sir Ralph nor his men-at-arms made any attempt to charge home against the Scottish spearmen.
(Angus McBride)

View from the Scottish position towards Redding Muir. In the valley bottom on the left is the site of the boggy loch. The left wing of the English army advanced down the slopes centre-left. (author's photo)

This well-preserved effigy of Brian Fitzalan (d.1306) is in Bedale church in North Yorkshire. He was on military service almost continuously between 1277–1302 against the Welsh and Scots. He fought at Falkirk in the brigade of the Bishop of Durham with six troopers. His arms, recorded by the Falkirk Roll were 'baree dor et de gulez.' (author's photo)

Presumably they feared that the Scots would attack and catch them unprepared. They urged the king to pre-empt any attack by the enemy and to take the initiative from them by an immediate onslaught of the heavy cavalry. 'So be it,' said the king, and he commended the impatient horsemen to the protection of the Holy Trinity. Wallace saw the movements of the horsemen on the distant hillside and knew that this was to be a day of battle and that the decision rested on the courage of his men. He urged his mount across the front of his troops and called out to them his famous rallying cry, 'I have brought you to the revel, now dance if you can.'

The English cavalry was organised into four brigades or 'battles', of this we can be sure, but we don't know whether the infantry was organised independently or whether each 'battle' was made up of a combination of horse and foot. Whichever is the case, and I incline to the former, the cavalry initially attacked without infantry support; it would be some time before the foot were up as many were still toiling along the road from Linlithgow. The earls of Lincoln and Hereford and Roger Bigod, the Earl Marshal of England led the cavalry of the vanguard. Their brigade led the attack and approached the Scottish position from the heights of Redding Muir, having crossed the Westquarter Burn in its upper reaches, before their progress was checked by the morass in the valley bottom. This episode caused some delay and confusion while the knights impatiently sorted

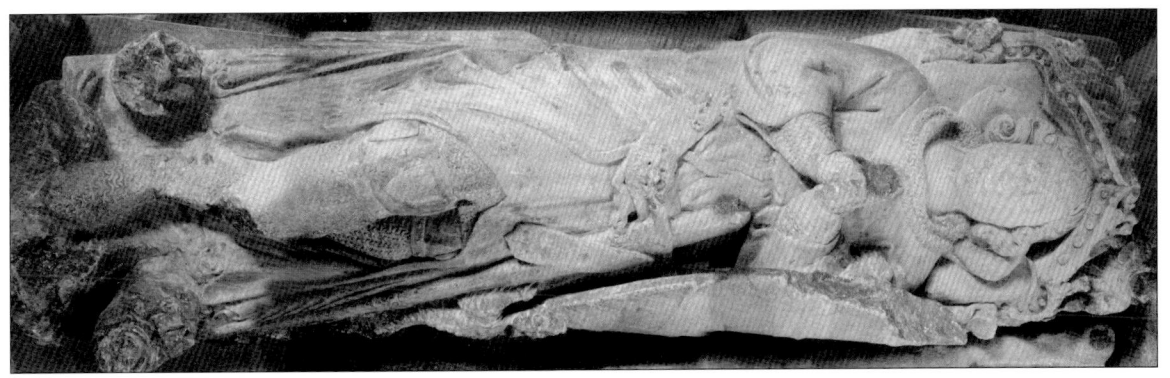

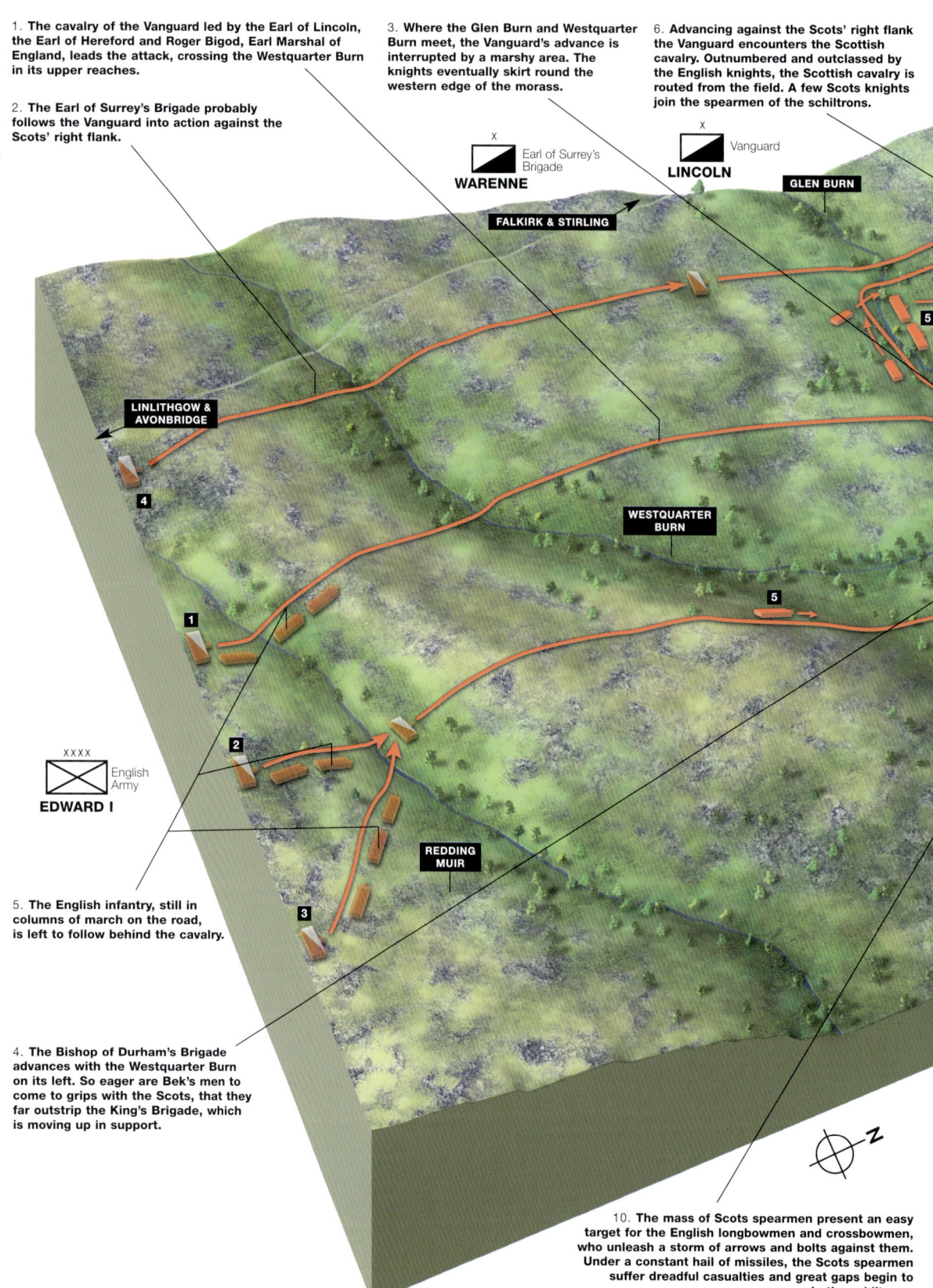

1. The cavalry of the Vanguard led by the Earl of Lincoln, the Earl of Hereford and Roger Bigod, Earl Marshal of England, leads the attack, crossing the Westquarter Burn in its upper reaches.

2. The Earl of Surrey's Brigade probably follows the Vanguard into action against the Scots' right flank.

3. Where the Glen Burn and Westquarter Burn meet, the Vanguard's advance is interrupted by a marshy area. The knights eventually skirt round the western edge of the morass.

6. Advancing against the Scots' right flank the Vanguard encounters the Scottish cavalry. Outnumbered and outclassed by the English knights, the Scottish cavalry is routed from the field. A few Scots knights join the spearmen of the schiltrons.

x
Earl of Surrey's Brigade
WARENNE

x
Vanguard
LINCOLN

GLEN BURN

FALKIRK & STIRLING

LINLITHGOW & AVONBRIDGE

4

WESTQUARTER BURN

5

1

xxxx
English Army
EDWARD I

2

5. The English infantry, still in columns of march on the road, is left to follow behind the cavalry.

REDDING MUIR

3

4. The Bishop of Durham's Brigade advances with the Westquarter Burn on its left. So eager are Bek's men to come to grips with the Scots, that they far outstrip the King's Brigade, which is moving up in support.

N

10. The mass of Scots spearmen present an easy target for the English longbowmen and crossbowmen, who unleash a storm of arrows and bolts against them. Under a constant hail of missiles, the Scots spearmen suffer dreadful casualties and great gaps begin to appear in the schiltrons.

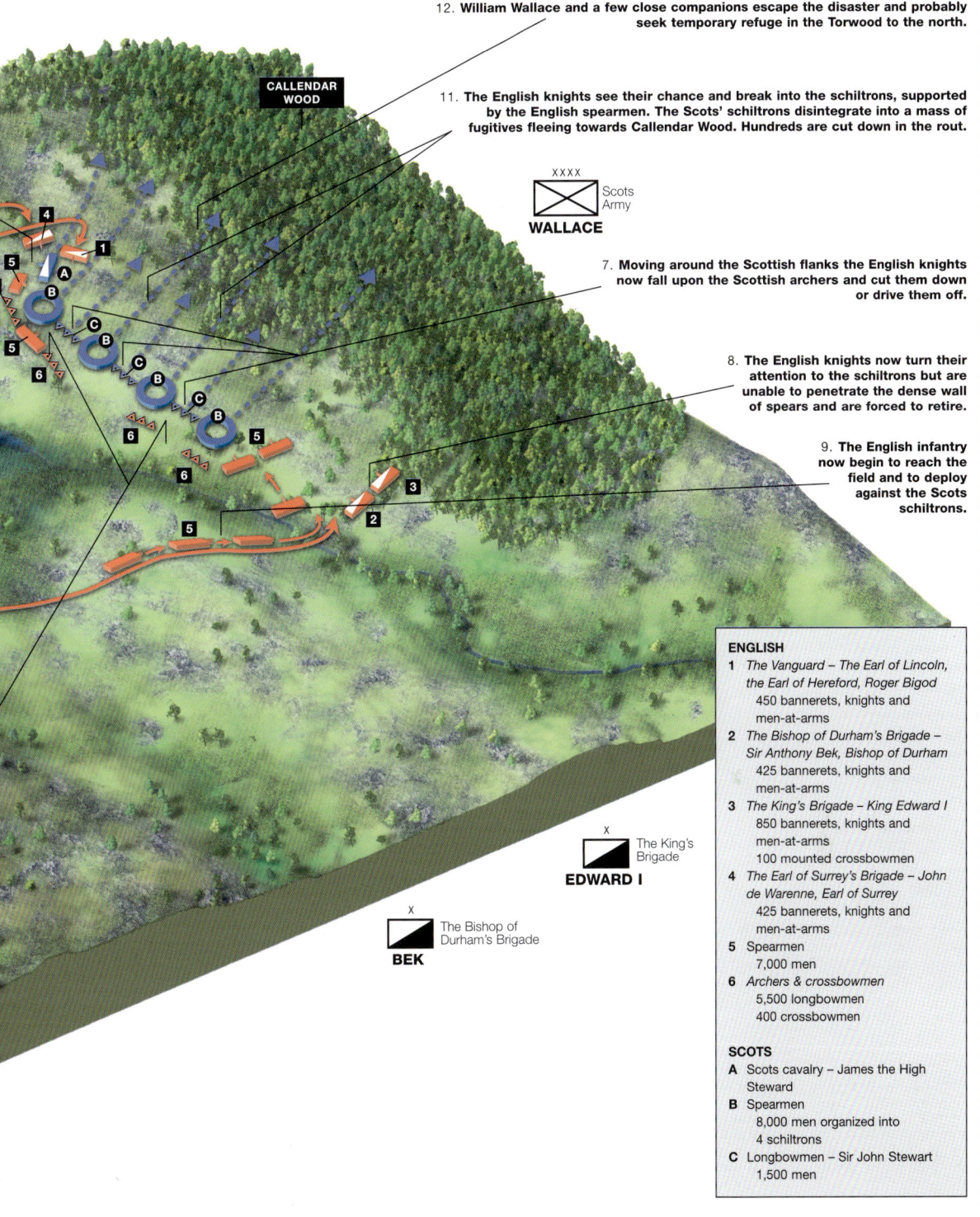

12. William Wallace and a few close companions escape the disaster and probably seek temporary refuge in the Torwood to the north.

CALLENDAR WOOD

11. The English knights see their chance and break into the schiltrons, supported by the English spearmen. The Scots' schiltrons disintegrate into a mass of fugitives fleeing towards Callendar Wood. Hundreds are cut down in the rout.

xxxx
Scots Army
WALLACE

7. Moving around the Scottish flanks the English knights now fall upon the Scottish archers and cut them down or drive them off.

8. The English knights now turn their attention to the schiltrons but are unable to penetrate the dense wall of spears and are forced to retire.

9. The English infantry now begin to reach the field and to deploy against the Scots schiltrons.

x
The King's Brigade
EDWARD I

x
The Bishop of Durham's Brigade
BEK

ENGLISH

1 *The Vanguard – The Earl of Lincoln, the Earl of Hereford, Roger Bigod*
450 bannerets, knights and men-at-arms

2 *The Bishop of Durham's Brigade – Sir Anthony Bek, Bishop of Durham*
425 bannerets, knights and men-at-arms

3 *The King's Brigade – King Edward I*
850 bannerets, knights and men-at-arms
100 mounted crossbowmen

4 *The Earl of Surrey's Brigade – John de Warenne, Earl of Surrey*
425 bannerets, knights and men-at-arms

5 *Spearmen*
7,000 men

6 *Archers & crossbowmen*
5,500 longbowmen
400 crossbowmen

SCOTS

A Scots cavalry – James the High Steward

B Spearmen
8,000 men organized into 4 schiltrons

C Longbowmen – Sir John Stewart
1,500 men

THE BATTLE OF FALKIRK

22 July 1298, viewed from the southeast, showing the advance of the English cavalry that, although unable to make any impression on the schiltrons drives off the Scots cavalry and archers. Now isolated, the Scots spearmen are easy prey for the English archers. As their tight formations begin to collapse the English knights and spearmen close in to finish the job.

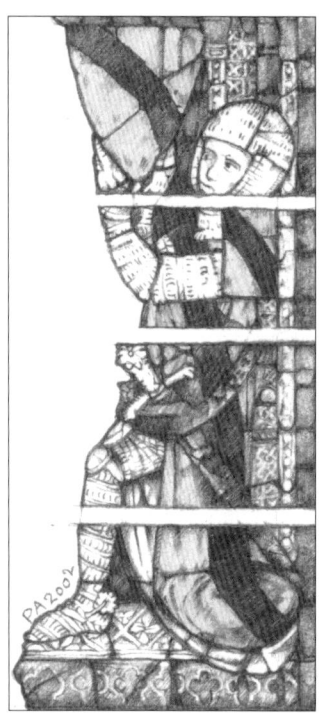

Piers de Mauley (1249–1308) from the Mauley window in York Minster. He served 1277–1300 against the Welsh, Scots and in Gascony. At Falkirk he fought in the brigade of the Bishop of Durham. (drawn by Pete Armstrong)

themselves out before skirting round the bog on its western side, but it had no effect on the course or outcome of the battle. This detour may have brought the vanguard directly into contact with the Scottish cavalry who were posted behind the flank of the schiltrons. Meanwhile, the second brigade of cavalry, commanded by Anthony Bek, Bishop of Durham with the earls of Dunbar and Angus was advancing with the Westquarter Burn on its left. It was alerted to the presence of the morass by the confusion of the vanguard and swerved eastwards to ride round the obstacle. In their eagerness to be first to come to blows with the enemy, Bek's horsemen far outstripped the supporting cavalry brigade behind, so the bishop himself ordered his knights to draw rein and await the approach of the third brigade, that of the king, rather than attack in a piecemeal manner. The bishop only had about 400 lances in his brigade; the king's brigade had about 800 men-at-arms, twice as many as any of the other three, and included a strong contingent of mounted Gascon crossbowmen; even combined, the bishop and the king's commands would have been outnumbered by a single schiltron. But the arrogant and impetuous knight, Ralph Basset of Drayton had no intention of waiting for the king and chided the bishop for his caution. 'It is not your office, bishop, to instruct us at this juncture in the art of war; you should rather concern yourself with mass. Go', he said, 'and celebrate mass if you will, for on this day we will do the fighting'. Ralph Basset's words epitomise the attitude of the majority of the English knights, notions of subordination and discipline had not yet permeated the ranks of the aristocratic horsemen and though their bravery and spirit were matchless, their ability to act in concert was at best uncertain. Bek's knights rode on, heedless of the bishop's attempts to restrain them, spurring their chargers towards the dark masses of spearmen on the slopes beyond. At the same time as the bishop's brigade came up with the schiltron on the left of the Scottish line, the Earl of Lincoln's brigade clashed with the cavalry stationed behind their right flank. The Scottish horsemen were outnumbered and outmatched by the English knights and were driven from the field in unseemly rout. So rapidly were they defeated that it seemed, at least in retrospect, that they fled the encounter without striking a blow. A few Scots knights however managed to find shelter inside the hollow schiltrons where they remained to fight and stiffen the defence. Later, there were accusations of treachery on the part of the aristocratic leaders of the Scottish cavalry, much of it aimed at the Comyns, but there is no evidence to support this notion for the Comyns were staunch bulwarks of the patriotic cause and the likelihood is that the charge stemmed from later attempts by Robert Bruce and his supporters to discredit his opponents.

Guisborough does not mention the part played by the fourth cavalry brigade which was led by the Earl of Surrey. However, we know that it took part in the fighting because of the record of horses killed belonging to the earl's knights. One of these was Aymer de Valence whose retinue included the sub-retinue of Thomas and Maurice de Berkeley; they must have been in the thick of the fighting as four of Aymer's troopers were killed and Maurice de Berkeley lost his valuable horse too. The probability is that the fourth brigade followed the vanguard into action west of the morass. Having put the Scottish cavalry to flight the English knights now turned on the formations of enemy archers. These the English knights caught in the open and destroyed without sustaining any real damage from their fire.

It seems that the horsemen, having ridden wide of the morass in the centre of the Scottish line, approached the schiltrons from the flanks rather than the front. With the archers deployed between the schiltrons, their view of the approaching horsemen was masked by the Scottish spearmen until the English knights wheeled round the rear of the schiltrons at the last moment. Lanercost describes the cavalry 'moving round and outflanking them on both sides' and Guisborough's account suggests the confused situation as the archers fought desperately, clustered in defence about the body of their leader, Sir John Stewart, who had been killed when he 'fell by chance from his horse.' The *Scalacronica* gives a different account of this incident and says that he had dismounted 'to fight on foot among the commons [and] was slain with more than ten thousand commons.' Having settled with the archers, the English knights then turned on the schiltrons of spearmen but were unable to break through the dense walls of spears. Their horses were vulnerable to the Scottish pikes despite their armour, and the horse lists, which have fortunately survived for Falkirk, show that 111 horses were killed. There is no corresponding record of injuries to the riders, but casualties do not seem to have been heavy, we know of only two bannerets who were killed in the battle. In the king's brigade Henry de Beaumont lost his own horse and three more from his retinue of ten, Robert Clifford lost eight out of 35 and the Earl of Lancaster 11 out of his large retinue of 45. Ralph Basset of Drayton's retinue of 12 knights and troopers, despite his insolent bravado, suffered no losses. He, like most of the cavalry, probably circled round the schiltrons probing for a weak spot. Horses will not, no matter how they are spurred on, charge home onto the points of spears. Being intelligent, sensitive animals rather than machines, they will invariably swerve away rather than commit suicide. A shower of bolts shot by the mounted crossbowmen galled the immobile Scots but their surviving bowmen, who had taken refuge within the schiltrons, returned a brisk fire that helped keep the horsemen at bay. The English cavalry were far outnumbered by the spearmen and, without the support of their infantry, they could not defeat them. Nor for that matter could the Scots, stripped of their cavalry and most of their archers, do much damage to the English cavalry. For the present there was an impasse. The English cavalry was not beaten, far from it, their casualties had been light and they had successfully put the Scottish cavalry to flight and destroyed their force of archers. The schiltrons were left isolated and apparently immobile, awaiting what seems, at least in retrospect, the inevitable.

John de Segrave (d.1325) fought at Falkirk in the vanguard with the Earl Marshal's retinue. He escorted the prisoner William Wallace to London in 1305 and was chief justiciar for his trial. (model by Pete Armstrong)

Aymer de Valence (d.1324) from his tomb in Westminster Abbey. He fought in the brigade of the Earl of Surrey at Falkirk where four of his retinue were killed. (author's drawing)

TRIUMPH OF THE BOWMEN

The stand-off gave the Scots a short breathing space before the onslaught of the English infantry. They had advanced in the wake of the horsemen, who drew back to re-form their ranks. The massed schiltrons of spearmen presented an easy target for Edward's archers who unleashed a storm of arrows and crossbow-bolts that decimated the forward ranks of the Scots. In addition to the archers, Guisborough tells us that 'some brought up round stones, of which there was a great plenty there, and stoned them.' We can't be sure that these men were dedicated slingers or simply infantrymen who took the initiative to pick up stones and add to the hail of missiles that was taking its deadly toll of the Scots. Gradually the

Knights of Robert Clifford's retinue in 1298. (Illustration by Lyn Armstrong)

Robert Clifford *Simon Clifford: who would have differenced these arms*	**Robert Haustede** *A tenant of the Cliffords*
John de Cromwelle *These are the arms of Vipoint: differenced*	**Thomas de Hellebek** *A Cumbrian knight*
Roger Kirkpatrik *A Scots knight of Auchen Castle in Annandale*	**James de Torthorwald** *A Scots knight killed at Bannockburn*
Richard Kirkbride *A Cumbrian knight*	**Robert l'Engleys** *Also recorded as a millinar of foot*

schiltrons, unable to reply to the barrage, began to waver and contract as men fell and the outer ranks were forced backwards on those behind. 'They fell like blossoms in an orchard when the fruit has ripened' wrote one English chronicler. As the deadly rain did its work, gaping holes appeared in the schiltrons and the English knights saw their chance and broke in among them, hewing down the spearmen at close quarters. Though Guisborough makes no further mention of the English infantry, the cavalry alone cannot have completed the defeat of the Scots, who would still have outnumbered them. The English foot, even allowing for the usual wastage, must have been at least as strong as the Scots infantry and would have included spearmen, in large numbers, who would have had some part to play in the final stages of the battle. A shred of evidence for the involvement of the infantry is provided by the horse lists, which record that the horses of John de Merk and William Felton, both millinars of infantry formations, were killed in the fighting. As the full weight of the English army was brought to bear against the Scots formations, they began to break up and men streamed away towards the rear; hundreds were cut down as they fled towards Callendar Wood. The only recorded English casualties of note were Brian de Jay, Master of the Templars and brother John de Sawtrey, Master of the Scottish Templars. One version of their demise has it that their horses became bogged down while incautiously pressing the pursuit and they were surrounded and killed in the woods; however, Lanercost says that the Master of the Templars was killed when he 'charged the schiltron of the Scots too hotly and rashly.' William Wallace, with a few of his closest companions, escaped the disaster and fled to 'castles and woods',

Seal of Eustace de Hacche (d.1306) who, with the two knights and nine troopers of his retinue, fought in the king's brigade at Falkirk where his charger, a bay with a white hind foot was killed. (author's drawing)

78

probably finding a temporary refuge in the Torwood, five miles to the north of Falkirk. When the English reached Stirling on 26 July they found barely a building habitable save the house of the Dominican friars where the king made his headquarters; Wallace had destroyed much of the town as he retreated north from the Torwood.

The Cost of Defeat

Contemporary chroniclers record huge losses among the Scots; the *Scalacronica*'s estimate of 'more than 10,000' killed is an exaggeration but within reason. Guisborough's 56,000 and Walsingham's 60,000 dead are preposterous and far exceed the number of Scots on the field though they may reflect the scale of the disaster and the high proportion of casualties, most of which were suffered by the common folk. For once a few of the names of the commons are recorded; they can be found in the archives at Durham. They are freeholders of Coldingham, in Berwickshire, who were either killed, wounded or forfeited their land for their part in the 'discomfiture' of Falkirk. Edward I ordered a series of forfeitures to take effect from 22 July, the date of the battle, clearly indicating participation in the affair. These indicate the presence at Falkirk of a section of the Scottish gentry, though only the High Steward among the great lords seems to have been present in person. The names of some Scots knights who fell at Falkirk are recorded; Andrew Murray of Bothwell and Macduff of Fife, James Graham of Abercorne, and Sir John Graham, whose tomb is in Falkirk churchyard along with a stone that marks the grave of Sir John Stewart, the Steward's brother, the manner of whose death is described above. Only the Templars, among those whose names were deemed worthy of recording on the English side, were killed. Losses among the English foot are not recorded but there is no reason to suppose that they were heavy.

AFTERMATH

Wallace after Falkirk

Wallace resigned the guardianship after Falkirk, his standing and the support of the nobility had depended on his military success and after his defeat they rapidly declined. His ascendancy had been brief and there could be no second chance. With no earldom or position of prominence to fall back on, Wallace once more became a figure in the shadows of history; the records allow us only occasional incomplete glimpses of his career in the seven years between the battle of Falkirk and his capture and execution. In 1299 Wallace went abroad to the French court on a diplomatic mission, evidently to canvas support for Balliol's kingship. He left Paris towards the end of 1300 with letters of recommendation from Philip IV to the Pope and presumably went to Rome. In 1303 Wallace was once more in Scotland, where he returned to the fray, though this time as one among several leaders of the struggle against the English.

Closing moves of the campaign of 1298

Edward I remained in Stirling after the battle for the next two weeks. Despite the scale of the defeat at Falkirk the battle was not decisive, the Scots were not subjugated, but it did mark the beginning of a grimmer phase of the struggle. The Scots were now fighting with their backs to the wall. Not for another 16 years would the Scots dare to meet the English in open battle. North of the Forth the Scots remained in control though Edward's raiding parties burnt their way across the country north of Stirling. Then as a result of MacDuff's support for Wallace they left a trail of destruction through Fife as far as St Andrews. Stirling Castle once more fell into English hands at this time and was not retaken by the Scots until late in 1299. The English raided Perth but the Scots burned the town themselves and withdrew before the English arrived. The English army was still having supply difficulties and Edward was still at loggerheads with a section of his barons who continued to make difficulties and wrangle over his delay in confirming the charters. The Earl Marshal and the Earl of Hereford departed, taking their feudal contingents with them, as they had a right to do. This left Edward with little choice other than to withdraw from Scotland. Stirling Castle was hastily repaired and garrisoned before he moved south by way of Falkirk and Torphichen. He was at Glencorse south of Edinburgh by 20 August. The king turned west at this point and marched to Ayr, intending to settle with the rebels of the south-west. He reached the town a week later but found it empty and burnt and the castle slighted, on Robert Bruce's orders, so that it would be of no further use to the English. Edward had expected supply ships from Ireland to meet him at Ayr but they failed to arrive and Guisborough tells us that 'For fifteen days there was a great

The ruins of Torwood Castle stand in the ancient Torwood north-west of Falkirk. Wallace and his remaining followers would have crossed the River Carron at Larbert, two miles to the south, to take refuge here after their defeat. (author's photo)

OPPOSITE **In 1298 Edward I built a wooden 'peel' at Lochmaben to tighten his grip on Annandale. In the Middle Ages Annandale offered the only practical route north on this side of the country and the castle at Lochmaben stood guard over it. (author's photo)**

EDWARD I'S SCOTTISH CAMPAIGNS 1300–07

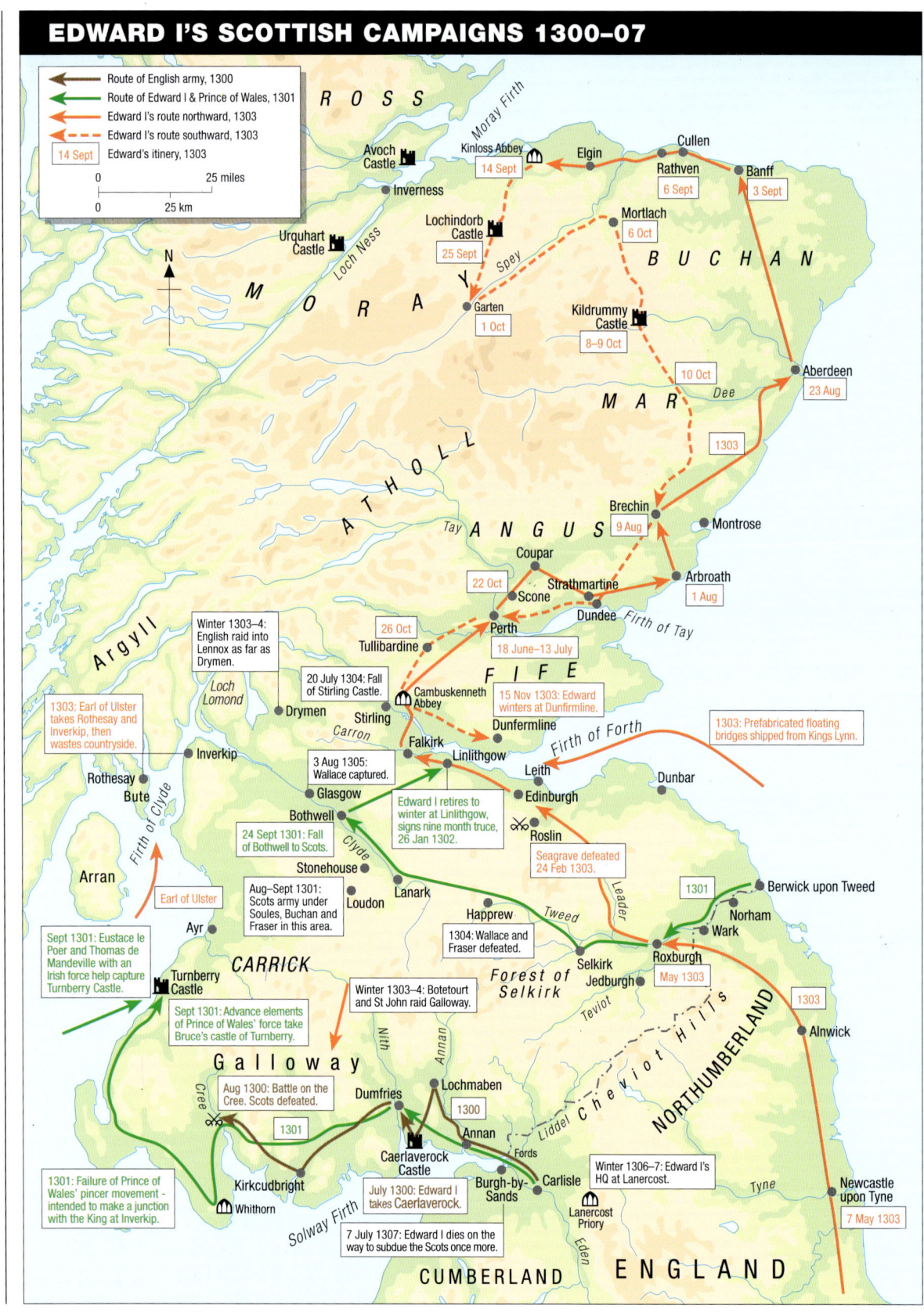

Legend:
- → Route of English army, 1300
- → Route of Edward I & Prince of Wales, 1301
- → Edward I's route northward, 1303
- →‑ ‑ Edward I's route southward, 1303
- 14 Sept Edward's itinerary, 1303

0   25 miles
0   25 km

N

R O S S

Moray Firth

Avoch Castle

Kinloss Abbey — **14 Sept**

Elgin

Cullen

Inverness

Rathven — **6 Sept**

Banff — **3 Sept**

Urquhart Castle

Lochindorb Castle — **25 Sept**

Mortlach — **6 Oct**

B U C H A N

M O R A

Loch Ness

Garten — **1 Oct**

Spey

Kildrummy Castle — **8–9 Oct**

M A R

10 Oct

Aberdeen — **23 Aug**

Dee

A T H O L L

1303

A N G U S

Brechin — **9 Aug**

Montrose

Tay

Coupar

Strathmartine

Arbroath — **1 Aug**

22 Oct

Scone

Dundee

Firth of Tay

26 Oct

Tullibardine

Perth — **18 June–13 July**

F I F E

Winter 1303–4: English raid into Lennox as far as Drymen.

20 July 1304: Fall of Stirling Castle.

Cambuskenneth Abbey

15 Nov 1303: Edward winters at Dunfermline.

1303: Prefabricated floating bridges shipped from Kings Lynn.

1303: Earl of Ulster takes Rothesay and Inverkip, then wastes countryside.

Loch Lomond

Drymen

Stirling

Carron

Dunfermline

Firth of Forth

Falkirk

Linlithgow

Leith

Dunbar

3 Aug 1305: Wallace captured.

Glasgow

Edinburgh

Edward I retires to winter at Linlithgow, signs nine month truce, 26 Jan 1302.

Roslin

Seagrave defeated 24 Feb 1303.

Rothesay

Bute

Inverkip

Bothwell

24 Sept 1301: Fall of Bothwell to Scots.

Clyde

Firth of Clyde

Arran

Stonehouse

Loudon

Lanark

Happrew

Tweed

Selkirk

Roxburgh — **May 1303**

Berwick upon Tweed — **1301**

Norham

Wark

Earl of Ulster

Aug–Sept 1301: Scots army under Soules, Buchan and Fraser in this area.

1304: Wallace and Fraser defeated.

Jedburgh

Forest of Selkirk

Leader

Ayr

C A R R I C K

Sept 1301: Eustace le Poer and Thomas de Mandeville with an Irish force help capture Turnberry Castle.

Turnberry Castle

Sept 1301: Advance elements of Prince of Wales' force take Bruce's castle of Turnberry.

Winter 1303–4: Botetourt and St John raid Galloway.

Teviot

Cheviot Hills

Liddel

NORTHUMBERLAND

1303

Alnwick

G a l l o w a y

Cree

Aug 1300: Battle on the Cree. Scots defeated.

Dumfries

Lochmaben — **1300**

Nith

Annan

1301: Failure of Prince of Wales' pincer movement - intended to make a junction with the King at Inverkip.

Kirkcudbright

Whithorn

1301

Caerlaverock Castle

July 1300: Edward I takes Caerlaverock.

7 July 1307: Edward I dies on the way to subdue the Scots once more.

Annan

Fords

Burgh-by-Sands

Carlisle

Winter 1306–7: Edward I's HQ at Lanercost.

Lanercost Priory

Eden

Tyne

Newcastle upon Tyne — **7 May 1303**

Solway Firth

CUMBERLAND

ENGLAND

82

Caerlaverock Castle, built in the late 12th century by Aymer Maxwell, is superbly situated on the Solway coast in Dumfriesshire. The castle is triangular in plan with towers and a massive gatehouse at the corners, all surrounded by a wet moat. (author's photo)

famine in the camp.' The army turned south despondently and trailed across the miles of barren moors into Nithsdale, then on to Lochmaben where Robert Bruce's castle was captured. Edward garrisoned the castle and spent time ensuring that the defences of both Lochmaben and nearby Dumfries were in order for he had no intention of abandoning that part of Scotland still under his control. Robert Clifford was left in charge of Lochmaben while Edward moved on to Carlisle, where he arrived on 9 September. Losses of horses in Scotland had been particularly high and the eight-week campaign had been hugely expensive. Edward had won a great victory but Scotland was not conquered and the campaign had yielded few results. In Carlisle Edward distributed the forfeited lands of the Scots who had opposed him in battle among his followers as a reward for their services. Many of these estates were still in Scottish hands and the English nobles to whom they were awarded would, as Edward well knew, have to support him again in Scotland to gain possession. The castle at Jedburgh was still in Scottish hands and Edward made a diversion there to supervise the siege before returning south towards the end of October.

SCOTLAND, 1298–1307

Late in 1298 Robert Bruce, Earl of Carrick and John Comyn the younger of Badenoch were elected as joint Guardians of Scotland but this arrangement was short-lived and the guardianship devolved on a succession of leaders, of whom the Comyns were invariably in the

forefront. Despite divisions within the leadership and the country itself the national struggle against English domination continued unabated in the name of King John. The only parts of the country still under English domination were parts of Dumfriesshire and the south-east of Scotland where English-held castles clustered more closely than elsewhere.

At the end of 1298 while still in the north, Edward I issued a summons for troops for a campaign in 1299 but this did not materialise and it was not until the summer of 1300 that he returned to Scotland. The campaign of that year aimed at prising loose the grip that the Scots had in the meantime re-established on the south-west of Scotland. Caerlaverock Castle was besieged and captured, after which the king advanced into Galloway and confronted a Scottish army led by the Earl of Buchan and John Comyn of Badenoch on the River Cree. In the ensuing battle the Scottish cavalry, which seems to have made up a large proportion of their army, was once again soundly defeated. Edward regretted that he had no Welsh troops with him to pursue the fugitives into the wild country where they fled and took refuge. In 1301 Edward I launched a further campaign in Scotland with the intention of taking and holding the natural line formed by Tweeddale and Clydesdale. The army invaded Scotland in two divisions, the larger, under the king, advanced from Berwick. The smaller force, under Edward of Caernarvon, now Prince of Wales, advanced into the south-west so that, in his father's words, 'the chief honour of taming the pride of the Scots should fall to his son.' The two forces were intended to carry out a pincer movement and effect a junction at Inverkip. However.

vigorous resistance by the Scots, combined with desertion among the foot prevented this and the prince was forced to retire to Linlithgow where his father had established his winter quarters. In January 1302 Edward I agreed a nine month truce with the Scots and when this expired he summoned troops to assemble in May 1303. In the meantime his lieutenant in Scotland, John de Segrave, set out to raid into a Scottish-held part of Lothian to the west of Edinburgh. On 24 February 1303 near Roslin the leading brigade of Segrave's poorly co-ordinated force was surprised and routed, with serious casualties, by a Scottish mounted force, whose leaders, it is thought, included William Wallace. Segrave was wounded and captured and, though the second brigade came up in the nick of time and rescued him, the affair was very nearly a major disaster and the Scots took heart from the encounter.

An End to the Business, Scotland 1303–1304

Edward I set out from Roxburgh in June 1303 with a strong cavalry force and about 7,000 foot, aiming 'to make an end of the business.' Previous summer campaigns had failed to subdue the obstinate Scots. This time the king intended to keep an army in the field all year round, as he had when he tamed the Welsh, and to allow the Scots no respite. At huge cost, three pre-fabricated pontoon bridges were built and transported in a fleet of 27 ships. Edward advanced into Scotland in easy stages, 'on every side he burnt hamlets and towns, granges and granaries… unsparingly.' The Earl of Ulster with troops from Ireland captured the

The square motte of the castle of Sir John Graham, who fell at Falkirk, is well-preserved and sited on the slopes of Cairnoch Hill, overlooking the Carron Valley about eight miles south-west of Stirling. (author's photo)

castles of Rothesay and Inverkip in the west, then turned to plundering the surrounding countryside. The Scots were unable to field an army equal to confronting the English in battle, they could only snap at their heels as they advanced relentlessly. The floating bridges were probably in place across the Forth early in June, allowing the English army to by-pass Stirling Castle and march north to Perth and then to Kinloss on the Moray Firth, where the king received the submissions of the northern magnates. The king returned by a circuitous route through the mountains to Dunfermline where he spent the winter months of 1303–04. Edward still had a sizeable army in the field and operations continued throughout the winter; a raiding force over 1,000 strong penetrated into the Lennox as far as Drymen; John de Botetourt and John de St John raided Galloway in strength, with four bannerets, 141 men-at-arms and 2,736 infantry. Troops commanded by Segrave, Clifford and Latimer surprised and routed a Scottish force led by William Wallace and Simon Fraser at Happrew in Tweeddale.

The small Scottish army led by John Comyn of Badenoch made several forays against the English from their base in the mountains, but their situation was desperate and, realising that defeat could bring ruin and an end to Comyn power in Scotland, the laird of Badenoch sued for peace. Edward's terms were lenient and the Scots submitted. In return they were granted life and liberty under their old laws and freedom from forfeiture of their lands. A few prominent rebels were singled out for temporary banishment, among them John de Soules, the guardian, who preferred permanent exile in France. No terms were offered to William Wallace, the king's enemy, who remained defiantly at large despite every effort on Edward's part to capture him. That he could do so reflects the popular support he could still rely on.

The siege of Stirling Castle

William Oliphant, the governor of Stirling Castle asked Edward's leave to send a messenger to John de Soules to ask what terms the castle might be surrendered on. The king refused the request and on the 22 April the siege of the castle began in earnest. It was a social as well as a military occasion and the king had an oriel window constructed in his town house so the ladies of the court had a comfortable vantage point. The most imposing array of siege artillery ever assembled in Scotland was brought to bear against the defences, but the garrison held out despite the fury of the bombardment, though eventually they were forced to surrender unconditionally for want of provisions. A rather comical addendum to the affair was added by the king, whose powerful new engine 'Warwolf', built on site at great expense, had not yet come into action. The King insisted that the siege was not over, nor were any of his troops to enter the castle 'till it is struck with the Warwolf, and that those within defend themselves from the said wolf as best they can.'

Capture and execution of Wallace

By the summer of 1304 Scotland was firmly in Edward's grasp, the castles were garrisoned with his troops and order was restored. The king returned to England with his army and the royal administration left York and returned to London; Edward was never to set foot in Scotland again. He appointed his cousin, John of Brittany, Earl of Richmond as his lieutenant in Scotland and, with political acumen, made sure that the Scots themselves played a large part in the administration of the country. Wallace was still at large but the net was closing and the king urged the Scots nobles to 'exert themselves…to capture Sir William Wallace, and hand him over to the king who will watch to see how each of them conducts themselves so that he can do most favour to whoever shall capture Wallace, with regard to… expiation of past deeds.' Wallace was captured on 3 August 1305 by a fellow Scot, Sir John Menteith. He was taken to London and led, crowned mockingly with laurel, in procession with the judges appointed to try him to Westminster Hall amid huge crowds who turned out to see the spectacle. The judgement, like the trial, was a formality and Wallace was condemned to a barbaric execution. He was dragged through the streets to Smithfield bound to a hurdle. There he was hanged, cut down while still alive and disembowelled, his entrails burned before him by the executioners. He was finally beheaded and his head displayed above London Bridge. What remained of his body was cut into quarters to be exhibited in Newcastle-upon-Tyne, Berwick, Stirling and Perth.

Death of Edward I and the resurgence of Scotland under Bruce

For Edward I matters in Scotland appeared finally to be settled. However, on 10 February 1306 Robert Bruce murdered John 'the red' Comyn of Badenoch in the Greyfriars Church in Dumfries and made himself King of Scots. On 7 July 1307 Edward I died at Burgh-by-Sands on the Solway coast on his way north to once more hammer the Scots into submission. He was succeeded by his son, Edward of Caernarvon, who was crowned King Edward II, but his interests were far from Scotland and the sorely pressed Bruce was given a breathing space in which to establish his rule, defeat his opponents and prise loose England's hold on his kingdom.

THE BATTLEFIELDS TODAY

There is still much of interest that relates to the battle to be seen about the town of Stirling though the site of the battle, in the loop of the River Forth, is now covered by the housing of the suburbs of Cornton and Causewayhead. From the ramparts of Stirling Castle,

A stone effigy originally marked Sir John Graham's grave but, as the sculpture mouldered to decay, other stones were placed over him bearing some record of his virtues and his fall (at Falkirk). In 1860 the present elegant railing and gothic cupola were added, though the sword that surmounted the tombstone, a replica of the mighty brand supposedly wielded by the hero himself, has disappeared. (author's photo)

where the Earl of Surrey saw the Scots forming their battle array below the Abbey Craig a mile away, the same airy view over the site of the battle can be enjoyed. The line of the causeway that led across the wet meadows towards Causewayhead below the Abbey Craig can clearly be recognised from the castle. Below is Old Stirling Bridge, which is now a footbridge. This medieval stone structure replaced the original late-13th century wooden bridge which stood a few yards upstream. The remains of the submerged piers of this early structure survive below the surface of the river to mark its position. Stirling Castle and the National Wallace Monument on top of their respective rocky eminences are the prominent landmarks of Stirling, both are interesting visitor attractions in their own right and remain the focus for an understanding of the topography of Wallace's victory. A hundred yards or so south of the Wallace monument is the spot, above the precipitous crags of the Abbey Craig, where Wallace and Murray deliberated their plans on the morning of the battle. Their troops were arrayed along a line now marked by those streets of Causewayhead below that run roughly parallel to the vantage point. The ford of Drip (NS770956) has long ago been replaced by a stone bridge. That near Kildean (NS776955) just above the high point of the tide is now the site of a motorway bridge; there is no possibility of fording the river here now and presumably the area is much changed since Wallace's day. A trip into the hills west of Stirling can be rewarding, perhaps visiting the picturesque site of Sir John Graham's castle (NS682858) above the Carron Valley Reservoir. The drive back to Stirling along the unfenced minor road across the fells offers extensive views and an appreciation of the impassable nature of these uplands that gave the castle and bridge at Stirling such strategic importance. The Smith Art Gallery and Museum on Dumbarton Road is worth a visit whilst in Stirling; there are artefacts relating to Wallace and the town in medieval times.

If the by-road that leaves the A872 and follows the course of the old Roman road towards Falkirk is taken, then the remains of the Torwood can be seen on the high ground to the south-west. The site of the battle of Falkirk is still a matter of conjecture and likely to remain so. Possible locations include the Loch Ellrig site, the rising ground east of Mungal Farm, the Polmont hills, the Hills of Dunipace and the Woodend or Westquarter Burn site. The latter is the site proposed in this book. This location fits the facts of the battle as far as we know them and despite encroaching housing, roads, a railway and a canal the basic features of the battlefield are still recognisable. A footpath leads down to the wooded junction of the Westquarter and Glen Burns at NT903783, then rises to a bridge over the Union Canal from where a panorama of the battlefield unfolds. On the ridge across the valley can be seen Woodend Farm, in the centre of what would have been Wallace's line of schiltrons. On the crest of the ridge is Callendar wood, which extends across the skyline. Below Woodend, in the valley bottom, though masked from this position now by the railway embankment, was the boggy loch or morass where the two Burns met; part of the site is now occupied by a small housing estate. Behind the viewpoint is the hillside leading up to Redding Muir; the Earl of Lincoln launched his attack down this slope, followed by John de Warenne. None of the possible sites around Falkirk have been examined systematically for evidence that might help locate

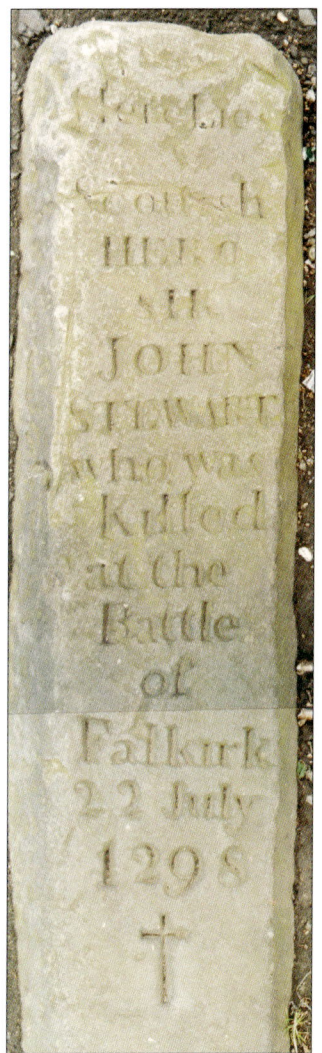

ABOVE **The last resting place of Sir John Stewart is marked by a recumbent stone that, until the mid-19th century, bore no inscription. (author's photo)**

OPPOSITE **The relief panels that flank the Wallace Monument in Elderslie, Renfrewshire, celebrate the hero's exploits in a ponderous, romantic style. Albert Hodge's heroically posturing 'men in mail-kilts' may seem risible to modern tastes yet the monument remains a fine example of Edwardian street furniture on the grand scale. (author's photo)**

the battlefield and the same is true of the site of the battle of Stirling Bridge. All the sites mentioned have been disturbed in the course of building and other work but no evidence has ever surfaced. Grave pits are the largest feature of a medieval battlefield that might be expected to survive, but none have been located; not even a single rusty spearhead or the tip of an arrow has turned up. This may be due to the damp climate and to soil characteristics in Scotland that together break down human remains quickly and cause ferrous artefacts to rust even quicker; it is unfortunately a story common to all Scotland's medieval battlefields.

High above the Westquarter Burn on Redding Muir, about a mile and a half distant stands the Wallace stone, or rather the obelisk that replaced it, in the village now named after it. The original stone disappeared long ago, probably chipped away by souvenir hunters. It was a large boulder on which, traditionally, Wallace was said to have stood to spy out the lie of the land thereabouts. It remains a fine vantage point to do just this; the view is extensive, though it doesn't quite seem to tie in with the battle of Falkirk. In the old part of Falkirk, known as Grahamstown after Sir John Graham who was killed in the battle, stands the ancient parish church of Falkirk where the memorials to Sir John Graham and Sir John Stewart, who also fell in the battle, are to be found.

SELECT BIBLIOGRAPHY

Scalacronica by Sir Thomas Gray of Heton, trans. Sir Herbert Maxwell (Glasgow 1907, reprinted Llanerch Publications 2002)

The Chronicle of Lanercost, ed. & trans. H. Maxwell (Glasgow 1913, reprinted Llanerch Publications 2002)

The Chronicle of Walter of Guisborough, ed. H. Rothwell (Camden 3rd series lxxxix, 1957)

Some Feudal Lords and their Seals (1903, reprinted Crecy Books 1984)

Falkirk Roll 1298 (The Heraldry Society of Scotland 1981)

Armstrong P. *The Battles of Stirling Bridge and Falkirk, Heraldry, Armour and Knights* (Keswick 1998)

Barrow G.W.S. *Robert Bruce and the Community of the Realm of Scotland* (Edinburgh 1988)

Blair C. *European Armour* (London 1958)

Chancellor J. *Edward I* (London 1981)

Fisher A. *William Wallace* (Edinburgh 1986)

Hamilton of Gilbertfield, William. *Blind Harry's Wallace* (Edinburgh)

Humphrey-Smith C.R. *Anglo-Norman Armoury Two* (IHGS 1984)

Hunter Blair C.H. 'Northern Knights at Falkirk, 1298', *Arch. Aeliana 4 xxv*

MacDonald W.R. *Scottish Armorial Seals* (Edinburgh 1904)

MacKay J. *William Wallace, Brave Heart* (Edinburgh 1995)

McNamee C. *The Wars of the Bruces* (East Linton 1997)

Moor C. 'Knights of Edward I', *Harleian Society Vols. 80–84* (London 1929–32)

Morris J.E. *The Welsh Wars of Edward I* (Oxford 1901, reprinted Llanerch Publications 1994)

Morris J.E. 'Cumberland and Westmorland Levies in the time of Edward I and Edward II', *CWAAS ns.iii* (1903)

Ross D.R. *On the Trail of William Wallace* (Edinburgh 1999)

Traquair P. *Freedom's Sword* (London 1998)

INDEX